Women in Mayo 1821–1851

Minor Thesis submitted to the
Department of Education University College, Galway.

In part fulfilment of the requirements of the
Degree of Master of Education of the National University of
Ireland Galway, August 1986.

1. Fuel for School from *The Graphic*, December 27th, 1879.

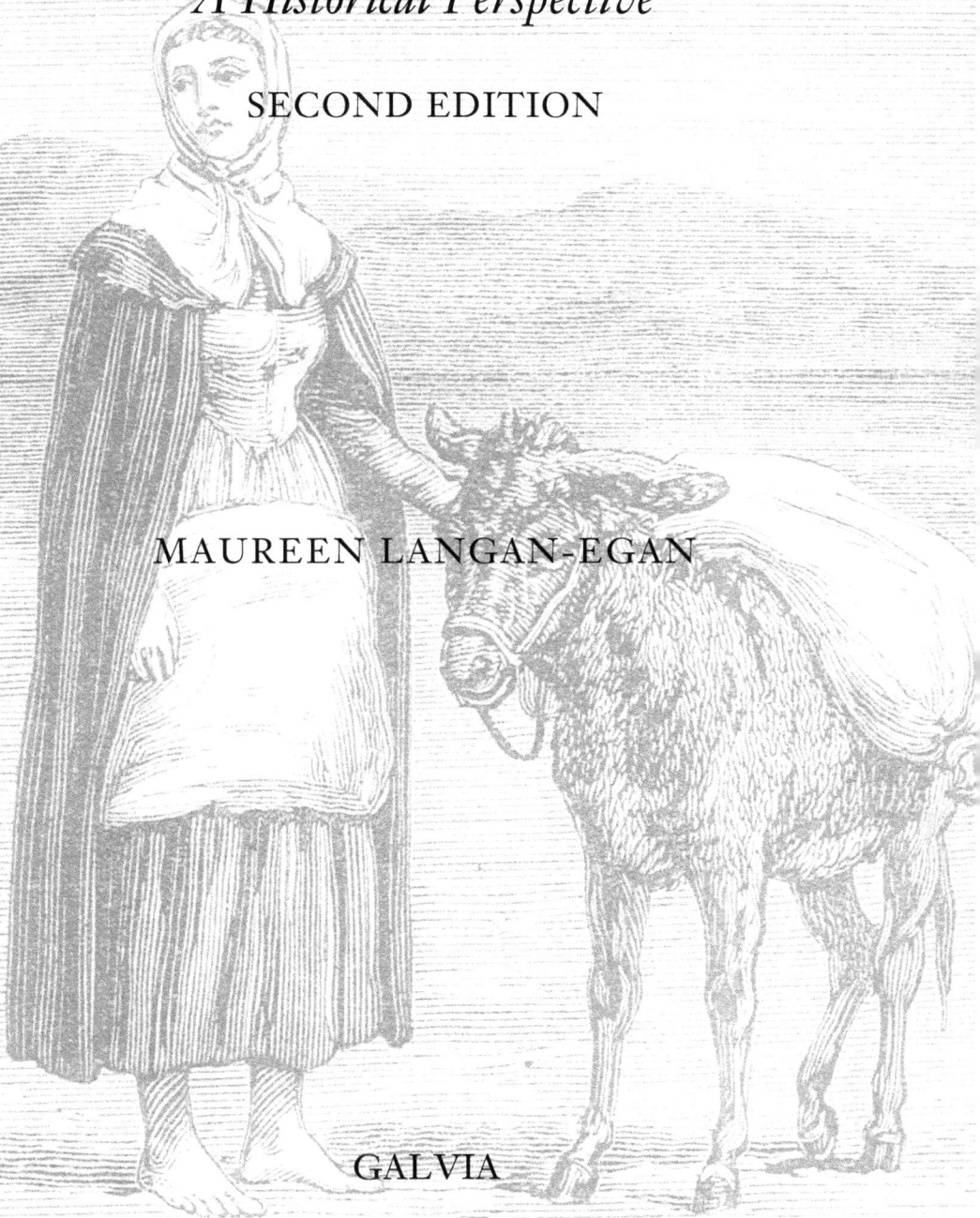

Women in Mayo 1821–1851

A Historical Perspective

SECOND EDITION

MAUREEN LANGAN-EGAN

GALVIA

Revised edition published by
GALVIA
Galway, Eire.
email: maureenlanganegan@yahoo.ie

an Irish imprint of CARRIGBOY
Wells, Somerset, England.
www.carrigboy.co.uk

First published in 1999 by OPEN AIR an imprint of FOUR COURTS PRESS.

A catalogue record for this title is available from the British Library.

Print ISBN 978-1-910388-18-1
ePub eBook ISBN 978-1-910388-19-8

Also available as a Kindle eBook from Amazon.com

This book was set in 10.5pt on 14pt Janson by
Carrigboy Typesetting Services.
Printed by CreateSpace.

Contents

2. Series of sketches depicting Mayo Peasantry, *Illustrated London News*,
November 20th, 1880.

Acknowledgements

I would not have succeeded with this thesis without the assistance of very many people.

It was my good fortune to have Dr T.P. O'Neill as my Tutor. His unfailing good sense, good humour and erudition eased my work considerably. I wish to pay tribute to an t-Athair Ó h-Eideáin, who was a guiding light for the duration of the course. The Parish Priests of Foxford, Crossmolina and Kilfian graciously granted me access to Parish Registers. As I perused these Registers, it was my privilege to meet Mr Tony Donohoe of Castlehill, Ballina; his guidance assisted me greatly when deciphering much of the handwritten material. The Sisters of Mercy, Ballina and the Sisters of Charity in Foxford helped me greatly. Sr Maura Flynn in Ballina examined the Convent Archives and provided me with much information concerning the early years of the Convent. Sr Agnes in Foxford provided me with a short synopsis of the history of the foundation using material from the archives and also lent me some rare published material. The Staffs of the University College, Galway (UCG) Library and of the Mayo County Library in Castlebar, especially Ivor Hamrock and Richard Hickey were unfailingly helpful. The staff of the State Paper Office in Dublin greatly facilitated my study of crime. Dr Sarah Pender of Placerville, CA, provided me with much relevant knowledge on the history of Ballycroy.

Miss Sandy Lawson produced the final draft of the Thesis at very short notice, which was first published by Berry Press in Westport, County Mayo.

I wish to record my debt of gratitude to Josette Prichard of Carrigboy for her interest, guidance and professionalism, which has been of such assistance in getting this work published. I could not have asked for better.

This book has been revised, with some updating prior to the publication of this edition.

Finally, I am indebted to my sons, Bernard and Gerard, and especially to my husband Bernard for his great patience, while this work was being completed. I owe much to the women of Mayo, whose story this is.

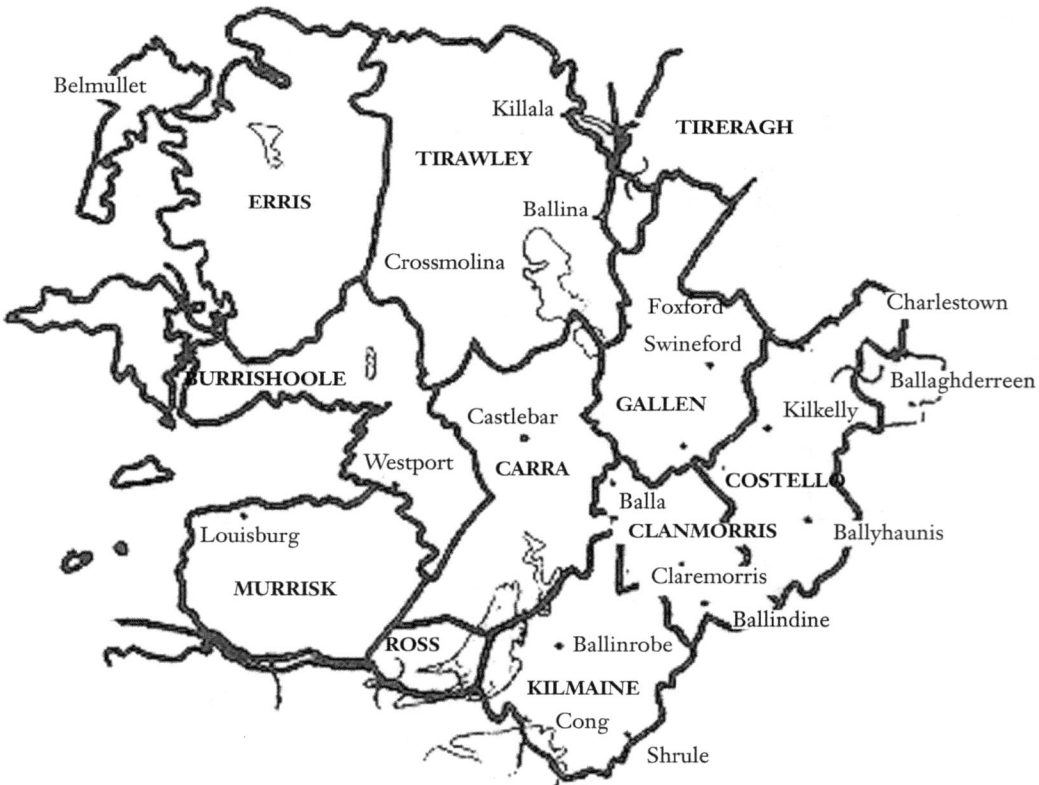

3. Map of Mayo showing Baronies and Main Towns.

Introduction

Ireland was fairly prosperous in the early years of the nineteenth century; high prices were obtained for agricultural products to supply the demand generated by the Napoleonic Wars. The end of these wars in 1815 marked the beginning of a dismal period which lasted to about 1845, just prior to the Great Famine. It has been described as a 'true Thirty Years War to the Irish people, a struggle between their vital needs and the interests of the landlords and moneylenders'.[1] This period is framed by two Censuses in 1821 and 1851. While doubts have been expressed regarding the reliability of certain aspects of the 1821 Census, it still provides valuable information on many relevant aspects of Irish life. The 1841 Census which reveals many changes and new trends is of particular interest as it depicts the situation in the country a few brief years before the Great Famine. Reference is made to it frequently in this research.

Ireland was marked by fluctuations in poverty in the period. Rapid population growth, low productivity in saleable goods and over-dependence on the potato as a staple food have been blamed for this situation. In truth, the country was badly affected by structural unemployment. The marked decline in industry noted caused great poverty, as many industrial workers including part-time workers were farmers and women.

At a time when women's incomes contributed much to family well-being, female unemployment depressed family income to a critically low level in subsistence areas, including much of Mayo, which did not have improving landlords, migrant labour or remittances from emigrants. There was much disguised unemployment as textile industries declined after 1815. Ireland had been able to supply its textile requirements in 1800 but by

---

[1] Strauss (1951), p. 118.

1830, the industry was in terminal decline; tariffs were lifted in 1826, allowing cheaper imports. Yet, many people were unable to afford the cheaper goods and frequently relied on migrant workers called *troggers* who bought cheap second-hand goods, often woollen goods, overseas to supply them with affordable clothing.

The sharp decline in cottage industry reduced the demand for labour, adversely affecting many people already afflicted by poverty. The loss of supplementary income meant that many could only pay the high rents by adopting the twin strategies of selling *poteen* (illicit whiskey) and by reducing living standards; for some this meant that 'potatoes were eaten at every meal and through all the seasons of the year'.[2] The residual skills which remained were used, however, by several relief organizations to provide permanent relief during the Great Famine.

The disorganised agricultural system added to the difficulties of rural dwelling. The *conacre* system (*see* Addenda) caused extra poverty and tensions in rural areas. Much tillage was carried on by the intensive use of the spade in growing potatoes on the seriously misnamed 'lazy-bed system' which, in fact, involved five times as much labour as ploughing and was 'a massive soak for surplus, under-employed labour'.[3]

Over 60% of holding comprised between 1–5 acres in Connacht in 1941. On such holdings, families constituted a type of dual economy, consisting of subsistence and fuel and cash crops. Even worse off, as they were trapped by over-dependence on land, were the landless and near landless labourers and particularly the *cottiers* (*see* Addenda).

A few more prosperous farmers got involved in the sale of butter, fresh eggs and slaughtered meat to industrial cities in England; they were able to avail of the new developments in transport, including coach roads, the railways and steamship services, all of which also played important roles in Migration and Emigration.

---

2   Appendix D, p. 243.
3   Whelan (1995) pp. 22–6.

Sadly, towns which might have provided employment did not develop as quickly as might have been expected, as the introduction of new technologies was hampered by ultra-conservative attitudes. The little progress made was too little, too late and very unevenly spread, particularly in the West of Ireland, including County Mayo.

County Mayo, situated in the Province of Connacht, is the third largest of the 32 Counties of Ireland in area. It contains large physical differences; much of North Mayo has poor subsoils, with large tracts of Atlantic raised bog. The South of the County has a largely limestone landscape. Achill Island is Ireland's largest island.

The County consists of nine historic Baronies, four in the North and five in the South (*see* Barony Map above on p. 8).

In the north, there are:

1　ERRIS, with Belmullet as its largest town
2　BURRISHOOLE in West Mayo, which contains Achill, Mulranny and Newport
3　GALLEN, which contains Bonniconlon and Foxford
4　TYRAWLEY (Tirawley), with the towns of Ballina, Ballycastle and Killala.

In the south, there are:

5　CLANMORRIS, with the towns of Claremorris and Balla
6　COSTELLO contains Kilkelly and Ballyhaunis
7　MURRISK, which contains Westport, Louisburgh and Croagh Patrick, (which with Ballintubber and Knock form three of the country's noted pilgrimage sites)
8　KILMAINE, contains Ballinrobe and Cong
9　CARRA, which contains Castlebar, the County Town and Partry

Ballina and Westport functioned as important ports. Larger towns in the county were market towns.

Many visitors to the County were inspired by its great variety of beautiful scenery, while bemoaning the lack of employment which they saw as a major cause of poverty. This led to stereotyping in many instances, with some being described as 'lazy wretches, who prefer beggary to work'.[4] While this statement may contain a small germ of truth, the fact is that many people spent their lives in an unremitting search for paid work and in unremitting toil (often unpaid) in an effort to survive.

Much information used in this research is contained in Parliamentary Reports and Papers, Famine Relief Papers, Parish Registers and Newspaper Reports. The Reports of various Commissions were of great interest, as witnesses gave accounts of their own lives or responded to questions put to them by Royal Commissioners. Reading them, one not only learned about their lives, one also got to know many of them as real, live characters. One learned of their thoughts, attitudes, hopes, aspirations, difficulties and struggles. One can only admire their coping strategies as they dealt with the extraordinary difficulties of their lives. It has been my privilege to have learned much about them.

Many unanswered questions regarding aspects of womens' lives remain, including that of unemployment. One wonders how several women coped when they were unemployed and lacked adequate resources to support themselves. Here, one encounters one of the many silences of Irish history. Was there some kind of support system among women, which enabled them to support each other through periods of unemployment? This seems probable, as much of their employment was seasonal. However, I found no evidence of such a system.

---

4   Beaumont de (1839), cited in N. Mansergh, *The Irish Question, 1840–1921*, London (1995), p. 24. De Beaumont thought the Irish slothful, deceitful, intemperate and violent. Quite frequently, foreign observers especially accounted for Irish poverty in terms of the people's laziness: they were indolent, they made no effort, neglected their land, their dwellings and their personal appearance. For a fuller discussion of this topic, see C. Maxwell *Country and Town in Ireland under the Georges*, London (1940) and Bertram Hutchinson 'On the Study of Non-Economic Factors in Irish Economic Development' in *The Irish Economic and Social Review 1:4 July 1970* pp. 513–9.

Many payments to women at this time were in barter or payment in kind, not cash. There is no doubt that some standard of measurement of value of work existed, which governed payment for labor in kind or by exchange of services. I have not found evidence of what standards governed these payments, how much they varied from place to place or how common these practices were in different areas. In fact, the practice continued in some areas long after the period under discussion. Many women may have been dissatisfied with this system; part of the attraction of money wages for them was that cash furnished a precise measure of value.

Many lives in Mayo were greatly affected by migration. There is little knowledge about how people's personal lives were affected by this practice. No reasons have been given why so many women from particular districts migrated, a practice almost unknown in other parts of the county. Both Achill and Erris were seriously impoverished at this time, however, the practice of migration was dramatically different in both Baronies being widespread in Achill and not so in Erris. No direct evidence of transhumance was found. Was this practice so widely accepted that knowledge of it has been forgotten?

In Education, the role of voluntary teachers is unclear. In 1826, there were 436 of them in the County. We do not know how many of them were women, what role they played in the schools, as they far outnumbered the number of people classified officially as teachers in that year. One wonders who appointed them, what subjects they taught and what remuneration they received?

The only constant in many women's lives was change – from 1815 to 1851 and, in later years, it must have seemed to many that the changes taking place in so many aspects of their lives were detrimental, adding considerably to the difficulties of their lives. In this context, one can only admire how so many rose to the challenges posed and survived, working hard to survive all their adverse experiences and struggling to build better lives for themselves and their families, whether at home or abroad.

4. Series of Sketches re. Boycott, *The Graphic*, November 20th, 1880.

List of illustrations

PICTURES CREDITS

Map of County Mayo showing Baronies and Main Towns, supplied by Ivor Hamrock, Local Studies Librarian, Mayo County Librarian, Mayo County Library, Castlebar, County Mayo.

Saunder's Newletter.

Illustrations 5–6, 8–9, 11–12, 15–16, 18, 22–23, 28–29 are courtesy of the National Library of Ireland.

Illustrations 13 and 21 are courtesy of Carmel Clancy of Ballintubber and Galway.

Illustrations 24–27 are courtesy of Eamonn O'Boyle, Ballina <image@eamonn oboyle.com>.

Illustration 20 is from Michael McLaughlin, <michael@michaelmclaughlinstudios. com>.

Illustration 30 is from a Private Collection.

Illustrations 31–32 are courtesy of Mr. Leonard of Bofeenaun.

Illustrations from *The Graphic* and *The Illustrated London News* are courtesy of Mayo County Library. I am indebted to Richard Hickey, Senior Executive Librarian for his expert knowledge of this material.

Cover photograph: Visitor to Achill (1911) leading a donkey, with barefoot children being carried in the traditional párdóga (panniers) used to carry turf.

I

Housing

When one considers housing in Mayo, one gets a general picture of small, dark congested cabins, often smoke-filled, generally consisting of one room[1] with rarely a partition.[2] Housing was of particular importance in women's lives, not only because the house was home, but was also the workplace for many women, forced to spend so much time in it. Women cared for their families and tried to earn any income possible from home by spinning, weaving or egg production. While there were notable differences in the buildings which functioned as cabins and in the materials of which they were composed, work done by most women in Mayo was carried out in dark, airless cabins, which were sources of continuous annoyance and frustration.

Areas such as Ballinrobe and Castlebar[3] had some cabins with two rooms and appeared relatively affluent. In areas, including much of Erris, people lived at the lowest level of human misery and degradation, in cabins often open to wind and rain. Nevertheless, the over-all size of the cabins was very small, even in areas with superior accommodation.

Some precise details as to size are available. In Ballintubber,[4] they were generally 20'–25' long and 10' or 12' wide. In Ballinrobe, they extended from 12' to 14' to 16' in width and from 20' to 30' in length.[5] These were much larger than those in

---

[1] Appendix E, p. 40.
[2] Society of Friends: *Transactions*. Account of William Bennett, p. 162.
[3] Supplement to Appendix E, p. 20.
[4] Supplement to Appendix E. Evidence of Fr. John Kirby re Borriscarra and Ballintubber, p. 20.
[5] Op. cit. Evidence of Courtney Kenny, p. 24.

poorer places such as those at Murrisk, which were 12'–18' long and about 12' wide.[6]

Better quality housing was generally found in the Ballinrobe area where rents had been reduced in 1823, unlike the rest of the county where exorbitant rents were the norm. In Cong, cabins were built of limestone,[7] as in Islandeady, where they were usually waterproof.[8] Sometimes, these were dashed.[9] In Ballinrobe, 'houses were built of limestone generally plastered inside with mortar and clay. Some have chimneys'.[10] Thomas J. Burgh, Dean of Cloyne[11] was impressed by the fine stonework of the cabins there. Women in these areas lived in comparative luxury, when contrasted with women living along the western seaboard. The poorer the dwelling the less likely it was to be waterproof or to have a chimney. They were 'hovels of the most wretched description'.[12]

In general, the cheapest building material available locally was used, including mud or mountain sods, others used loose stone with mud or clay to close the chinks, as at Kilfian and Rathrea.[13] A mixture of loam and earth was used in Dunfeeney (Doonfeeney) and Kilbride.[14] In another part of that parish 'There are many (cabins) with sods and banks of turf some cut out of the bank of turf with bog-scraws'.[15]

Apart from Erris, Kilvine and Crossboyne had the worst housing. The cabins there consisted of 'some sods piled one over the other, stone without mortar, plastered with cow-dung and clay in order to make them somewhat warm; people were quite unable to purchase lime for that purpose'.[16] Later, it was said that

---

6   Appendix E, p. 40.
7   Supplement to Appendix E. Evidence of John Flynn, p. 24.
8   Ibid. Evidence of Rev. P. Ward, p. 19.
9   Ibid. Evidence of Theobald Burke, Esq., p. 19.
10 Ibid. Evidence of Courtney Kenny, p. 24.
11 Ibid. Evidence of Thomas J. Burgh, Dean of Cloyne, p. 24.
12 Ibid. Evidence of C.A. Taylor, Civil Engineer, p. 19.
13 Ibid. Evidence of Rev. Michael Conway, p. 29.
14 Ibid. Evidence of Rev. Francis Little, p. 29.
15 Ibid. Evidence of John Faussett, J.P., p. 29.
16 Ibid. Evidence of Rev. David Jennings, P.P., p. 2.

5. Murrisk Friary, North window. This picture contains three ladies fashionably dressed and an elderly constable.

'human wretchedness seems concentrated in Erris'. The wall of the bog often forms two or three sides of the cabin while sods form the remainder and cover the roof',[17] an opinion supported by William Bennett[18] who wrote in 1847 that 'cabins were holes in the bog covered by a layer of turf and not distinguished as

[17] *Transactions*, James H. Tuke, 'An Account of his visit to Connaught in the Autumn of 1847'.
[18] Ibid. Letters of Wm. Bennett from Belmullet, p. 162.

human habitations from the surrounding moor until they close upon them'. Doorways, not doors, were usually found at both sides – back and front – to take advantage of the wind direction. A second apartment or partition was exceedingly rare.

Chimneys and windows were unknown particularly in the west of the county. In Erris, 'Window there is none, chimneys are unknown, an aperture in front some three or four feet in height serves the office of door, window and chimney'.[19] Chimneys were not always found in prosperous areas,[20] though windows and chimneys became more common as people became a little better off.[21] Unfortunately, if broken, these windows were not repaired and the openings were closed with mud with the passage of time.

To compound the general misery, many cabins were not waterproof. Some, as at Kilcommon, were open to wind and rain. Most stone cottages built at places such as Islandeady were waterproof.[22] because they were better built and had better roofing materials. Generally, though, poor quality material available locally was used for roofing, such as scraws and straw, as at Dunfeeney,[23] heath and rushes as at Killasser[24] and sods in Erris.[25] Even in Murrisk[26] with its many stone cabins, straw and potato stalks were used on roofs.

The locations of the cabins were generally most unhealthy, often built along the verges of bogs, on the most valueless land – a swampy piece of land was always selected to build them on for fear of wasting any land that might be productive.

In the aftermath of the Famine, one saw a dramatic decrease in the poorest form of housing, the so-called 'Fourth-class House' which was defined as an 'all mud cabin having only one room'.[27]

---

19 Ibid. Evidence of James H. Tuke, also Wm. Bennett, p. 162.
20 Supplement to Appendix E. Evidence of Courtney Kenny, p. 19.
21 Appendix E, p. 40.
22 Supplement to Appendix E. Evidence of Rev. Peter Ward, p. 19.
23 Ibid. Evidence of John Faussett, J.P., p. 29.
24 Ibid. Evidence of Rev. McNally, p. 23.
25 *Transactions*, evidence of James H. Tuke, p. 162.
26 Appendix E, p. 40.
27 Appendix A, Evidence of Mr. Doyle, p. 292.

For the county as a whole, by 1851 there was an increase of .7 (Vol. VI, Table XXV, 1851 Census) in the occupancy of First Class houses and of 4.6% of second class housing. A Second Class house 'comprised a good farm-house, or in towns, a house in a small street, having from five to nine rooms and windows'. First Class housing was adjudged to be 'all houses of a better description than a second type'. There was a dramatic increase of 33.3% in the occupancy of Third Class houses, with a decrease of 38.3% in the occupancy of the fourth class houses. This change marked a great improvement in living conditions, space available and lighting for those who moved into third class housing, as a Third Class house while 'still built of mud varied from two to four rooms and a window' in contrast with the Fourth Class house, which consisted of 'a mud cabin having only one room'.

There was a smaller percentage increase in the occupancy of Second Class houses in Mayo. This increase of 7.2% is understandable, because acquiring a Second Class house, whether in town or country, represented a large capital investment, unavailable to many people. The greatest mobility was shown in the increase in occupancy in the Third Class houses, an increase which was considerably higher than the average figure of 23.1% increase for Connacht as a whole and of 11.7% for the whole of Ireland. The decrease in the occupancy of fourth class housing was 7.1% greater in Mayo than for Connacht as a whole and was higher than for the whole of Ireland by 8.1% in 1851, yet numbers of people continued to live in this type of housing, which was frequently associated with small holdings of poor-quality land for many years to come.

Thus, for Mayo women, Famine survivors who retained their holdings, there was a marked change for the better in their accommodation in many instances.

Living conditions in cabins were deplorable, however, with a lack of furniture and household effects; although there were great differences within the County. Usually, districts with better housing had relatively better quality furniture yet there was a prevailing picture of deprivation.

Bedsteads were absent in much of the County, as in Kiltimagh where 'there were no such thing as bedsteads',[28] a fact also noted in Kilmaclash[29] and Murrisk.[30] Conditions were little better in Borriscarra and Ballintubber where people had 'no bedsteads and hardly any feather beds, straw being generally used.[31] Chaff was also used'.[32] Some ingenious devices were used to reduce the effects of damp on bedding. In Kilinna and Kilmaclasser, for example, 'generally beds of straw are placed on poles and supported at head and foot by stones to raise them from the damp of a floor'.[33] Conditions were much better in Castlebar, with two room cabins containing two bedsteads. One respondent was 'much surprised at finding in the smallest cabins at least one feather bed. The bedding is warm but their families being large are very crowded'.[34]

A clear account of sleeping arrangements in Murrisk shows a common pattern in the County. 'Where there is one bed in the house, it is occupied by the married couple of the house and their younger children. If the cabins contain but one room, the remainder of the family lie together on straw on the clay floor; if it contains two rooms it is generally that the females sleep together in the inner room where the married couple lie'.[35]

There was a lack of bed-clothes in most homes, with some having no bed covering whatever. 'I know many families, sometimes eight in number without a single blanket. People are covered by the tattered clothes which they wear',[36] read one account, which was supported by evidence from Kilinna, Kilmaclasser and Kilmore Erris, where 'bedding was extremely bad; in some instances none whatsoever'.[37]

---

[28] Supplement to Appendix E. Evidence of Myles McDonnell, p. 22.
[29] Ibid. Evidence of G.A. Taylor, p. 19.
[30] Appendix E. Evidence of Rev. M'Manus, p. 70.
[31] Supplement to Appendix E. Evidence of Rev. John Kirby, p. 20.
[32] Ibid. Evidence of Captain Ireland, p. 25.
[33] Ibid. Evidence of Rev. Myles Sheridan, p. 19.
[34] Ibid. Evidence of Lt. Col. James M'Alpine, J.P., p. 20.
[35] Ibid. Evidence of Rev. Mr. Dwyer (Murrisk), p. 70.
[36] Supplement to Appendix E, p. 19.
[37] Ibid. Evidence of Rev. Myles Sheridan, p. 19.

6. Ballintober (Ballintubber) Abbey in ruins.

In relatively prosperous areas, also, there was a general absence of bedclothes. John Flynn, Esq., J.P. had, prior to 1836, distributed 60 pairs of blankets and about 100 yards of flannel purchased for a sum remitted to him for the poor by a Mr. Tidman of London.[38] Quilts, of thin cotton material, so poor as to be sold new for 15d.[39] were commonly used among laborers.

---

[38] Ibid. Evidence of John Flynn, Esq., p. 24.
[39] Appendix A. Evidence of M. Loftus, p. 368.

There was widespread use of 'poverty blankets' – consisting of half-wool and half-tow.[40]

Available beds were not always given to girls. A doctor's report from a sick cabin stated: 'The only bed that was raised was given to the son, who was looked up to as the future support of the family; the mother and daughters lay two and two in straw beds spread on the damp floor'.[41]

As well as poor bedding, there was a general lack of furniture. In some cases, as at Kilmina, there was none.[42] William Bennett visiting Belmullet in 1847 stated: 'Furniture properly so called, I believe, may be stated at nil. ... I saw neither bed, chair nor table at all. A chest, a few iron or earthen vessels, a stool or two, the dirty rags and night coverings formed about the sum total of the best furnished'.[43] In Islandeady, with poor bedding, furniture in the cabins consisted of two or three pails and a large form, on which they (the people) sat.[44] In Kilmaclash, a straw bed and a stool or two were noted[45] but in Robeen, cabins had deal tables.[46]

Bedding, such as straw, was easily infested and a proper standard of hygiene was impossible to maintain. One account states: 'Their beds are in such a state from filth and vermin that to any one accustomed to cleanliness it is purgatory to approach them.'[47] Privies were quite unknown even to the more comfortable occupants of the mountains. 'All are filthy in the extreme even those who are above want and who could keep themselves and house clean'.[48]

Outside, many cabins were almost unapproachable from the mud and filth surrounding them; the same inside or worse, if possible from the added closeness, darkness and smoke.[49] While

40 Appendix A, p. 292.
41 Ibid. Evidence of Mr. Devlin, M.D., p. 291.
42 Supplement to Appendix E. Evidence of Rev. Charles Hargrove, p. 20.
43 Society of Friends: op. cit. Wm. Bennett, p. 162.
44 Supplement to Appendix E. Evidence of Theobald Burke, p. 19.
45 Ibid. Evidence of G.A. Taylor, p. 19.
46 Ibid. Evidence of J. Knox Gildea.
47 Appendix A. Evidence of Fr. Lyons, Kilmore Erris, p. 385.
48 Supplement to Appendix E. Evidence of Thomas J. Lindsay, p. 40.
49 *Transactions* Evidence of Wm. Bennett, p. 162.

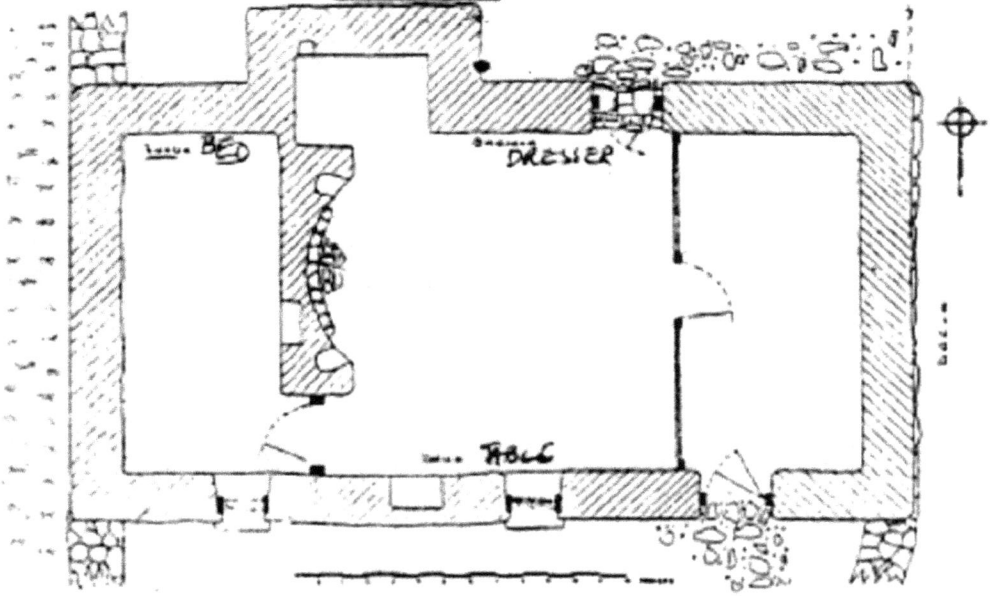
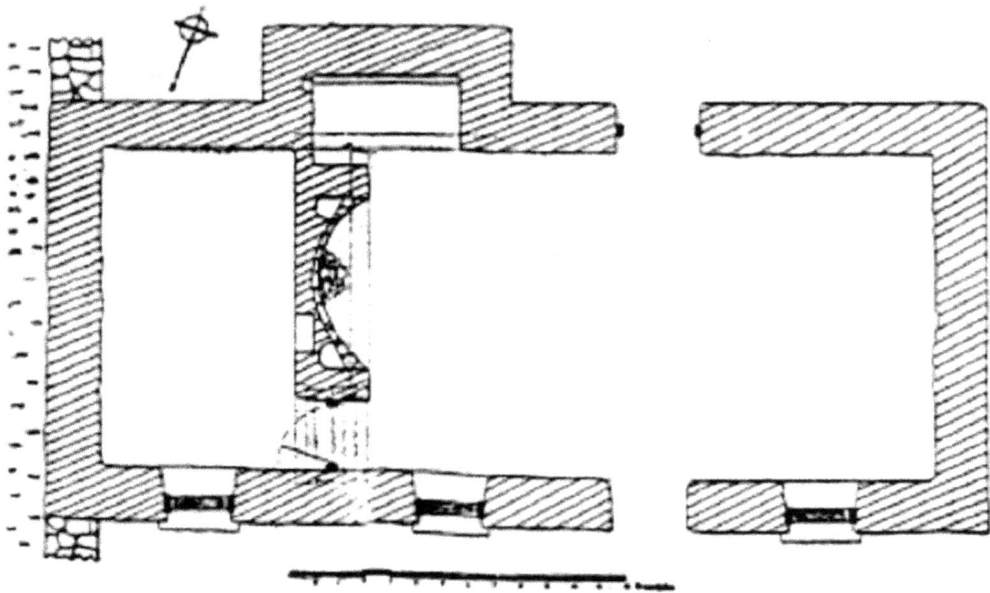

7. Diagrams of Typical Houses *c.*1838 by Sean MacGiolla Meidhre.
Tourmakeady, Co. Mayo.

dramatic improvements had taken place in housing by the end of the period under consideration, the available evidence shows that many women still lived in squalor because of grinding poverty.

Ake Campbell and Sean Mac Giolla Meidhre have given us some insight into the lives of women in the cabins. The two houses in the diagram situated at 7 Carheen, Tourmakeady were built about 200 yards from each other on the same street.

They represent a type of house very common in the Mayo area and show the usual arrangements in prosperous cabins. Both were of the straight gable type, with a *cailleach* or sleeping niche. This *cailleach* had a screen hung in front of it, in an attempt to give a measure of privacy to its occupants, a luxury which women in other parts of the County, such as Achill, did not have. Opposite the *cailleach* in the older house was a small nook in the wall, used to store clothes, etc.

(In other houses, clothes and wool were kept in bags hung from a hook in the wall). There is a fireplace in the sleeping room in the two houses and the beds were placed longitudinally along the wall opposite this fireplace. Unusually, there are window sills. The floors are earthen except for paving under the main fireplace.[50] The living arrangements in these houses were luxurious by contrast with those which obtained in Achill, with its many one roomed cabins, with no chimneys or windows.[51] Clay floors, which were the norm, added greatly to the burdens carried by the housewife, being unhygienic and impossible to keep clean. In Foxford, as elsewhere, they became sodden, especially in Winter, a condition often aggravated by leaking roofs. The hearth was often in the centre of the cabin; areas such as Foxford[52] had no grates, while in Tourmakeady, there was paving under the main fireplace.

---

[50] Mac Giolla Meidhre, Seán: 'Some notes on Irish Farm-houses', p. 196. In *Béaloideas*, Iml. VIII, 1938. Also Campbell, Ake. *Béaloideas*, Iml, V, No. 1, 1935.

[51] Newman, Edward: *Magazine of Natural History* quoted in *The Way that I Went*, p. 192.

[52] Finlay, T.A. *Foxford and the Providence Woolen Mills*, pp. 8–9.

While the hearth was the focus of the home, the lay-out of the cabins made life difficult for women. Keeping small children from falling into the fire was an ongoing challenge. Much squabbling occurred for the most comfortable place near the fire, particularly in cold, wet or frosty weather. There was chaos particularly when animals were allowed to roam freely, as in Foxford and Achill, where they had the run of the house. In parts of Foxford, a portion was sectioned off for the pig, which abated the nuisance somewhat. People were forced to keep animals inside, not just because the pig was a symbol of prosperity, but because 'there was no pig sty or any back yard in which the dung heap could be placed.'[53] The writer, William Sharman Crawford, bemoaned the fact that such cabins were being let to unfortunate tenants. On occasions, cows were kept in the house, or brought into the house at milking time. Hens were allowed the run of the house, though they were sometimes cooped up. They received particular attention when eggs were hatching. There was no stabling in which to keep them but even if there were, it is quite understandable that many women might not have used it for hens at this time on account of the difficulty of keeping clutches of incubating eggs sufficiently warm to hatch successfully.

One can imagine how difficult it was for many women to move around their cabins, particularly as so many of them were very badly lit. This may have been a result of the Window Tax, introduced in 1799 to pay for the war with France, which led to very small windows which allowed in a glimmer of light, often from the front of the house only, as people were afraid to instal too many windows, fearing increased rents. Thus, there was little light in many cabins, making it very difficult to accomplish any work, particularly close work such as spinning or knitting which require good light. Many windows were fixtures and could not be opened to admit air. This helped to contribute to the foul, unhealthy, musty atmosphere of the houses. While a through current of air could be generated by having two doors opposite each other, this was not the universal practice in cabin

---

[53] Devon Commission Part I, p. 131, 1847.

construction. In particular, people feared the night air which was believed to carry disease.

The use of a half-door was a boon for many women, serving to admit some light and air and also acting as a barrier both against animals or fowl, such as geese, seeking entry and against children wandering out, perhaps to fall into dung-heaps which were placed near the front door. Near the coasts, sea-sand was sometimes spread on the floors of cabins, which may have helped hygiene, but also reflected light.

Fowl such as hens and hatching fowl received great attention, the more so as they had come to provide almost the sole independent income that many women could earn which was regarded as the housewife's own. Eggs had been used as food for the family in better times, but in the period in question were being sold to pay rent or help to provide clothes for the family. It is possible that young goslings were kept inside until they were hardy, as the sale of geese provided income for women at Christmas. The theft of geese also figured in some court cases and women may have kept geese in to keep them safe. Goose eggs provided food for the family, particularly when women were forced to sell hens' eggs.

Cabins were hotbeds of disease. The incidence of illness added a nightmare quality to the lives of women who bore the burden of coping with family illness. The poor living conditions, poor food and poor clothing all contributed to the incidence of disease. Bad water supplies and the proximity of dung-heaps to the houses, which helped the spread of insect and fly-borne diseases, helped to make much illness endemic. It was very difficult, in particular, to keep babies and very young children healthy in such conditions and women came to dread illness, particularly the illnesses associated with Summer, long before the Famine.

Small pox was a major killer of young babies at 6 months, 9 months and 1 year. To complicate matters, the highest death rates from measles in young children occurred at the same ages. Croup killed many children in the first three months of life and

8. Westport Railway Hotel. Note car in the foreground.

then killed very few until they reached the age of 1. In 1841, croup killed 285 children at the age of 2 and 208 children at the age of 3. Mothers rightly dreaded convulsions in small children as they caused so many deaths. In 1841, they caused the deaths of 745 children at the age of 1 month and 305 children at the age of three months.

Women often dreaded Summer not only because so many of them had to beg at this time but because it was the main season for fever, which was a major killer between the ages of 6 and 60. Death caused by fever seemed particularly cruel as it killed many young people between the ages of 16–20 and women in the prime of life, particularly between the ages of 36–40 and 45–50.

Coping with such illness was made particularly difficult for women, not only on account of the utter unsuitability of the cabins as places in which to nurse a sick person, but because they usually could not rely on the help of their neighbors, so readily available in other circumstances. The dread of illness, particularly of fever, even kept family members away from a cabin so afflicted. It even affected those women forced to beg. We read that Hugh Moran's mother-in-law scarcely could get him to lie down fearing that the neighbors thinking he had cholera might take a disgust against her and not let her near them.[54] Even more difficult to cope with than intensive illnesses such as fever were wasting diseases, such as consumption, which killed many women between the ages of 26 and fifty, with the chief incidence of death occurring between the ages of 45–50.

Of the female ailments which were a particular worry, the chief was puerperal fever, caused by the lack of hygiene and dreadful living conditions. 301 women between the ages of 26–30 died of this fever in 1841.[55]

In normal times, women relied very much on each other's company, and were fond of visiting, particularly on Sundays. It seems to have been the universal pastime, and provided a great social occasion for storytelling, *béaloideas* (folklore), spinning parties, etc. In both 1841 and 1851, when the Census was taken on Sunday, there were more female visitors than male in the County. Tirawley had the greatest number of both male and female visitors and Clanmorris the least in these years. In 1851, there was a greater number of female than male visitors in every parish in the Barony of Tirawley except Ballycastle town. Moygownagh, which had a great number of widows, had twice as many female as male visitors. Women did not confine visiting

---

54 Appendix A, p. 499.
55 1841 Census, Table II, p. 168.

to houses or near neighbors as there were 1,157 listed as visitors to the Public Institutions in 1851.

Many liked to get away to the sea in Summer, and those forced to beg often went to places such as Murrisk to enjoy the sea-bathing, as well as to harvest carrageen and dilisk. In Winter, in the survival months, the main emphasis was on staying indoors as much as possible and it was now that the time by the fire was chiefly spent in story-telling, music, song, knitting and spinning.

Women at the time did not suffer from isolation or loneliness as houses were clustered together. Women actually complained of loneliness later on, when a pattern of dispersed farm settlement became common. There were snags attached to this closeness, however. There was much litigation caused by neighbors living too closely to each other. Many cases which came before the Petty Sessions involved petty squabbling among women, caused by trespassing, calling each other names, throwing dishwater into each other's faces, offences caused by women living under a great strain in ever worsening conditions.

While the concept of a certain amount of living space being necessary for both physical and mental health was unknown to poor women trying to stay alive against overwhelming odds, nevertheless the cramped, squalid living conditions must have caused great strain, if not mental illness, in the lives of several women. The greatest deprivation, however, suffered by many women was surely the complete lack of privacy, particularly in poorer areas such as Achill, where the cabins consisted of one room with no partitions.

Living conditions for women were very slow to improve. Conditions within the cottages in Fallmore (Belmullet area) in 1862 remind us that conditions had hardly changed except for the worse in forty years. The cabins were poorly thatched. The under-the-roof situation in this area was very difficult to cope with as the 'beds consist of a few sticks laid across two piles of stones and covered with a bundle of straw. The bed clothing is scanty and of the most wretched kind, often consisting of an old thin quilt, without any blankets. In every house I saw either a pig, a cow, or a donkey. In two of the houses into which I went, men were lying sick, and the fires that smoldered on the hearth could not afford warmth or comfort to the poor invalids.'[56]

Obviously, generations of women had lived their lives without ever having known decent living conditions. In other parts of the County, such as Foxford, matters were still as bad in 1890, where pigs were still commonly kept indoors and where people still lived in the most abject poverty in very small houses with one fixed window.[57]

One of the greatest challenges faced by women in the latter half of the nineteenth century was to have improved living conditions. By the force of example and teaching, the Sisters of Mercy and Sisters of Charity did much to help women to improve the quality of their lives as well as their health, often having to fight much ignorance and prejudice to do so.

The difficulties faced by women were aggravated by conditions within the cabins, their main workplaces. Working conditions for them could not have been worse. Lack of light and swirling smoke often meant that they could not see their work properly. There was a lack of storage facilities and thus any kind of container was valued by the harassed housewife. Damp, dirty conditions made it almost impossible to keep clothes clean and dry and, because of this, there was great emphasis on storing materials and clothes in bags above floor level, which kept them safe from smoke and moths. Those who were better off had chests to store blankets and some articles of clothing.

The struggle to keep the interior of the cabins clean was never-ending. The quality of bedding used meant that cabins were infested with lice, with the consequent suffering caused by itching, skin diseases and interrupted sleep. It was impossible to keep floors clean, especially when straw was used as bedding and when animals had the run of the house. If the housewife left the door of the cabin open, she was assailed not only by odors from within, but also by the foul smells which wafted from the dung-heap invariably placed near the front door.

---

[56] Saunder's Newsletter, pp. 218–219, 1862.
[57] Finlay, T.A., op. cit. p. 9.

Containers for smaller items in the cabins as well as containers for food were very important. Many women had a special box for needles. As salt was the only condiment or 'kitchen' which many people could afford with their potatoes, great stress was placed on keeping it dry. Thus, salt was stored near the fire. Baskets of all sorts were a boon because they could be made cheaply of local materials by the housewife or her family and were easily replaced, unlike cooking utensils, many of which had to be discarded when they were broken, because people could no longer afford to repair them. Potatoes were kept in large baskets and eggs in smaller ones. They were also used to bring meals to men in the fields and eggs to the market. Women in many parts of the County were familiar with the *cliabh*, or back-basket which they used to carry turf as in Achill, or seaweed as in Kilmore Erris. In the absence of other utensils, women often served food in baskets. Bread and potatoes were commonly served in this way.

After the Famine, such baskets often became symbols of poverty and the art of making baskets from straw or rushes almost died out until revived in the 20th century by the I.C.A. (Irish Countrywomen's Association). As with clothing, it became fashionable at the latter end of the period to procure the factory produced container and discard the home-produced article as being inferior.

It can be seen that the airlessness, darkness, smoke, penury, squalor and dirt, lack of space, poor cooking arrangements, poor utensils or their absence meant that the working conditions endured by women added considerably to the other burdens which they endured in their lives.

In retrospect, one can only pity the poor women who spent lives never knowing decent living conditions, never perhaps having a regular supply of good food, never having a proper change of clothes and never knowing any relief in their lives from the continual struggle against poverty and against the dreadful monotony of their lives.

9. Figure on fluted column. Female stone figure over plinth. Inscribed to the memory of George Glendenning, born in Westport 1770, died in Westport 1843. Mr Glendenning supplied data concerning the plight of unmarried mothers.

2

Clothing

J.G. Kohl, a German traveler, describing Ireland *c.*1840 stated:

> 'The rags of Ireland are quite as remarkable a phenomenon as the ruins. There is something quite peculiar in Irish rags. So thoroughly worn away, so completely reduced to dust upon a human body, no such rags are elsewhere to be seen'.[1]

This description is peculiarly apt for the clothing of people in Mayo in the period under consideration. Many people were unable to leave their cabins in Winter through the want of ordinary clothing.[2] In some cases, people attempted to supply the want of clothing by fire and were often obliged to supply that comfort by theft.[3] The Parish Priest of Murrisk estimated that the annual expenditure of any given number of the small tenantry on clothing and furniture did not exceed £1.[4] On holydays and when attending fairs or markets, the men were rarely without shoes or stockings; the women were very generally without either, but the children were always so. To keep up appearances on such occasions necessitated great efforts on the part of very poor people, as attested by one parish priest, 'When I go to a village to hold a station, one man comes and confesses to me and when he has done he gives his coat to his neighbor, that he may come in also; the very women do the same

---

1   J.G. Kohl describing Ireland *c.*1840, quoted in *The Irish in Scotland, 1798–1845*.
2   Appendix E. Evidence of Rev. Mr. M'Manus, p. 70.
3   Supplement to Appendix E. Evidence of Rev. M. Conway, p. 29.
4   Appendix E. Evidence of Rev. Mr. Dwyer, p. 70.

2. Series of Sketches depicting Mayo Peasantry, *Illustrated London News*, November 20th, 1880.

and change not only their cloak but their gown'.[5] Most people could not afford new clothes. Women endured great privations to provide clothing for themselves and their families. One lady[6] had 'coarse canvas out of old rice bags twisted around the children and not made into clothes as the material was so worn

---

[5]   Supplement to Appendix A. Evidence of Rev. Mr. Gibbons, p. 380.
[6]   Appendix A. Evidence of Mary Moran, p. 372.

10. Popular dress worn by young girls c.1880, showing cloaks, shawls, headgear. Shoes were worn by the better off.

it would not bear a stitch'. When going out to beg, a common plight among these women, many used to wrap a sheet about them and in one instance a piece of old carpet.[7] The woman in question did not use a blanket for this purpose as many did, as she had been obliged to cut the blanket in two for the family.

Heroic efforts were made to get any type of clothing: when beggars got a surplus of provisions they sold them to buy clothing. 'One woman bought a piece of coarse sheeting which served as a covering both at day and night'[8] Edmund Dixon of Kilmore Erris tells us how his wife procured a new coat for him. She begged the wool, bit by bit and spun it at home. She spent four months wandering about the country gathering it, about six pounds in all, begging at the same time for food for herself and her children.[9] His wife illustrates the great efforts made

7   Ibid., p. 367.
8   Ibid. Evidence of Fr. Gibbons, P.P., p. 504.
9   Ibid. Evidence of Edmund Dixon, p. 508.

to make clothes last as long as possible. 'She had a fine gown thirteen years old, which she spared for six or seven years. On a fine day she would lay it aside and do without a gown'.[10] Their daughter had to strive very hard to provide herself with a gown. 'She bought a little pig for 6d. The family were able to rear this on the refuse of potatoes for three months while the father was working. The pig was sold for 5s. 6d. and thus the girl was able to buy the gown'.

The want of clothing affected not only the appearance of the people but their attendance at school, church and their health. Many children in several areas were prevented from going to school 'by the want of sufficient clothing to cover their nakedness'.[11] Lack of clothing was a potent factor in spreading and prolonging illness, when people could not buy new clothes or cleanse the old ones, as sometimes they could not get soap; 'always their clothes were so patched that the art of Man could not wash them'.[12]

Many women depended on cast-offs to clothe themselves and their families. There are references to the operations of the Dorcas Society in Aughavale and Westport[13] whereby the poor by paying a trifle, when recommended by a subscriber could get a blanket, a gown or petticoat or other parts of a woman's dress. This society also operated in the Crossmolina area.[14] Some felt, however, that the poor, especially beggars, could not derive much advantage from that society.[15]

There was a great demand for second-hand clothes, particularly woolen goods, often sold at fairs and markets. Migratory laborers often tried to take advantage of this market to make a profit for themselves. In Scotland, there was a class of migratory Irish beggars called *troggers* who brought linen from Ireland

---

[10] Ibid. Evidence of Edmund Dixon, p. 508.
[11] Appendix A. Evidence of Rev. W. Hughes, P.P., p. 370.
[12] Ibid. Evidence of Pat McNamara, p. 367.
[13] Appendix E, p. 27.
[14] Ibid., p. 28.
[15] Appendix A, p. 493.

11. A view of Westport, a well-designed town showing the river bridge and a view of the Railway Hotel.

which they bartered for old woolen clothes,[16] which they sold or bartered in Ireland on their return.

In spite of the poor supplies, clothes were used as pledges in pawnbrokers' shops.[17] They were frequently pawned in April, May, June and July and redeemed after the harvest. It was not

---

[16] *Old Statistical Account* (999) 139/1793 quoted in *The Irish in Scotland 1798–1845*, p. 173.
[17] Famine Volume 4. 7th–8th Series 1847–1849. Evidence of Mr. R. Bourke, pp. 112–113.

uncommon for parties on their way to the workhouse to leave their best clothes with him (the pawnbroker) as pledges, stating that they were seeking admission to a workhouse and they thought their clothes were safer with him than elsewhere.

However by 1848, clothing had improved somewhat as wool prices had dropped and it was cheaper to produce better clothes. Nevertheless, the standard and quality of clothing had declined particularly since the latter half of the eighteenth century, when Arthur Young stated that 'the peasants were not ill-dressed on Sundays and holidays and that black or dark blue was almost the universal hue'.[18]

At that stage spinning was universal in all the cabins and people were able to spin and weave enough to clothe themselves with drugget for women and frieze for men. To realize how drab dress had become, a letter described the dress in Erris before the Famine. 'On days such as Sundays, before the Famine, the women were well and comfortably clad; red cloth cloaks, caps with gay ribbons, shoes and stockings (when at Mass or meeting), stiff gowns looped up, so as to exhibit a portion of a short red, or black, flannel petticoat completed the dress of the women'.[19]

While weaving and spinning had failed to provide employment, there is much evidence that these skills were widely used by women and girls to dress themselves up to the time of the Famine. A description of Erris life before the Famine is revealing in this context. 'Their scrap of tillage supplied them with abundance of potatoes, on their mountain land they reared cattle which furnished them with milk and butter and sheep which supplied all the wool they required for their coarse hand-made clothing'.[20] By the time of the Famine, the high prices of wool which obtained for a few years previously meant that people were not able to clothe themselves in woolen garments. With the desperation of starvation, many people were forced by necessity to kill off their remaining sheep, thus leaving them without any

---

18 Young, Arthur, *A Tour in Ireland, 1776–1779*. Volume II.
19 Famine, Volume 4, 8th Series 1849. Letter of George Crampton, p. 130.
20 Society of Friends: *Transactions*, Appendix III, p. 209.

12. Burrishoole Friary.

supply of wool. This was a great disimprovement from the point of view of clothing and blankets. To make blankets, cloth, called twill locally, had been woven as strips 27" wide on hand looms in the cabins. Then the individual strips were stitched together to form coarse blankets.

By 1847, William Forster spoke of the necessity of providing some coarse woolen garments for poor men and women.[21] Lack of such clothing was a contributory factor in the collapse of

---

[21] Wm. Forster: 3rd Jan. 1847. P.R.O.O. (l A, 42, 16).

many men and women on Famine Relief Works. Much clothing was collected both in England and in the USA to attempt to remedy the dreadful clothing situation in Ireland.

Migration also affected the weaving and spinning of garments at home. In 1845, it was reckoned that many people owed as many potatoes as brought them over to the next season and as much corn as would pay the rent and they went to England to earn as much money as might buy the clothing for their children.[22] As Mayo had a very high rate of seasonal migration, it was badly affected by this practice, as many people bought second-hand woolen clothes in England or Scotland before returning home, in order to eke out their meager savings.

Many Famine Relief Schemes employing women were based on their knowledge of spinning and weaving and we are told that in the Westport area, previous to 1846–48, every *cottier* (*see* Addenda) tenant or small farmer sowed a portion of flax every year, the manufacture of which kept the mother and daughters of the family usefully employed during the long winter nights. Some spun wool sufficiently fine to make dresses for themselves and frieze coats for their fathers and brothers,[23] and the spinning wheel not infrequently formed an important item in the marriage portion of the farmer's daughter.

After the Famine, weaving and spinning declined. The substitution of cash wages for the older *conacre* (*see* Addenda) system helped accelerate the decline as many people now began to buy all their clothing where it had been manufactured at home in poorer times. Saunders describes the new trend:

> 'You will rarely see a suit of home manufacture worn by any of the peasantry, either male or female, particularly the latter, who spend their earnings in the neighboring towns in the purchase of cotton dresses and striped petticoats and have quite got out of the system of making their own clothing'.[24]

---

[22] Devon Commission, Part I, p. 389.
[23] Saunder's Newsletters, pp. 1890, p. 90.
[24] Ibid., p. 191.

These skills had almost died out in the County when the Sisters of Charity came to Foxford in 1890.

Both before and after the Famine, feminine apparel in Mayo was characterized by bright colors, yet the standard of clothing had disimproved. Before the Famine, the women of Erris were dressed in good quality fabrics, dyed bright by the skillful use of vegetable dyes. After the Famine, while very many women, particularly the young, were dressed in bright hues, the standard of clothing had disimproved because now these ladies were attired in garments of poor quality material such as shoddy, mass produced by English factories.

It was to remedy the clothing situation as well as to provide employment that Mother Mary Arsenius,[25] who come to Foxford with perhaps four other Sisters of Charity in 1891, brought two hand looms, that had been used in Ballaghaderreen, to Foxford and set them up in an unused corn store. Thus, the tide began to turn slowly in favor of home produced superior quality cloth many years after our period.

That women felt very deeply about their poor clothing and lack of footwear is clear from the fact that, when they emigrated, they rarely went barefoot. They changed their habits with regard to dress more than in any other respect. For instance, when they obtained regular work in Scotland, they soon purchased 'showy clothes'.[26] Those, however, who had to resort to or enter workhouses overseas, such as that in Edinburgh, were very indifferent about their clothing. The trend towards better clothing was also noted in the USA, even though young Irish girls remitted a lion's share of their monthly earnings to Ireland.[27] Emily Skinner, writing from the Australian Goldfields, paid tribute to the adaptability of the Irish, as well as to their dress sense. She recorded:

---

[25] Correspondence with Sr. Agnes, Sisters of Charity, *Foxford Convent Records*.
[26] B.P. Papers, Vol. XXIV, Appendix G, page (xii).
[27] Nichols, T.L., *Forty Years of American Life* (1862).

'I guess they knew better long before this, for of all the people to adapt themselves quickly to a way of living better than they have been accustomed to, I never saw any equal to the Irish. Slips of girls who have scarce known shoes or stockings in a few months will develop into born ladies. I suppose there is a natural gentility in them'.[28]

Little has been recorded of the efforts made by Irish women overseas to help poor female family members who remained in Ireland to have good quality clothing. In particular, parcels from America containing fashionable items of clothing were very welcome. These were very helpful in providing 'the traditional Sunday best' and clothing for special occasions.

---

[28] Skinner, E., *A Woman on the Goldfields: Recollections of Emily Skinner, 1854–1878*, p. 59.

3

Food

The food situation in Ireland had become worse for several decades before the Great Famine, a situation aggravated by a great increase in population, high rents and the lowered value of the produce of the land. As a consequence, more and more women struggled to supply themselves and their families with food. The difficulties were intensified during particular periods such as Summer, particularly in July. These difficulties, which were experienced by most women irrespective of marital status, compelled very many to beg.

In no other aspect of life was the dreadful monotony of the lives of the poor so evident as in the matter of food. Trevelyan speaks of the Irish as 'living on the verge of human subsistence'.[1] The potato was the staple item of diet and it has been variously estimated that a man, his wife and three children would require from twelve to twenty four stones of potatoes in the week.[2] Great efforts were made to vary the diet for special occasions. 'The people are very desirous to have a little meat at Christmas and Easter and will make a sacrifice to obtain it ... half of the inhabitants of Clare Island did not taste meat last Christmas Day and I never knew said thing to occur in any other part of the country',[3] reported one correspondent.

Maintaining food supplies had become more difficult particularly since 1815. Fr. Michael Conway stated tersely that 'the condition of the poor deteriorated in stock, cash and comfort

---

[1]   Trevelyan, C.E., *The Irish Crisis*, pp. 7–8.
[2]   Appendix E. Evidence of John Kearns and John Burke, p. 5.
[3]   Ibid. Evidence of Rev. Mr. Dwyer, p. 5.

since 1815'.[4] Reductions in earnings added to the difficulty of providing food for laborers and the lower ranks of craftsman. By 1836, 'no little farmer or laborer, weaver or artisan could earn as much money in a week in 1815 as he does now in a month'.[5] While many reasons were given for the deterioration in living standards, such as the high price of land well below the produce of the land, excess rents,[6] increasing population and want of employment, the fall in the price of cattle, tithes, and grand-jury jobbing, one cause for the reduction in living standards must have occasioned great hardship to women in particular. This was the suppression of the linen trade.[7] Linen had kept all the females, both young and old, busily employed but by 1836 there was no employment for them except at harvest.

There were pockets, such as the Castlebar area, where the conditions of the poor had 'decidedly improved'.[8] Conditions in Ballinrobe and Cong were much better, where productivity had increased with the reduction in rents.[9] Notwithstanding these few notable exceptions, it is clear that living conditions had disimproved considerably over most of the county. The dependence on the potato as a staple food was deplored by thinking people, who stated: 'if the peasantry were enabled to make corn their chief diet, the periodical reoccurrence of distress in this county would be nearly stopped as a failure in the grain crops hardly ever takes place'.[10] However, this dependence on the potato was regarded in a different light by others and it was remarked that 'the fact that the cultivation of potatoes did render famines less likely elated the peasants who felt their increasing numbers to be a menace to the landowning classes'.[11] This seems

---

4   Ibid. Evidence of Rev. M. Conway, p. 25.
5   Ibid. Evidence of Thomas J. Lindsay, p. 25.
6   Ibid. Evidence of James McHale, p. 25 also Rev. P. Gibbons, p. 27.
7   Ibid. Evidence of Thomas J. Lindsay, p. 25.
8   Ibid., p. 40.
9   Supplement to Appendix E. p. 40.
10   Appendix E. Evidence of S. O'Malley, Bart, p. 5.
11   Ó Súilleabhain, Amhlaoibh. *Cinn-Lae Amhlaoibh Uí Shúilleabháin.*

to be a strange statement, when one realizes that partial famines or shortage of potatoes often drove women to beggary or to try to provide other substitute foods, which would feed themselves and their dependents. Not only was the over-dependence on the potato deplorable but, in the period under consideration, people lived on a type of potato called a 'lumper' which would have been designated animal food fifty years previously. These potatoes which required less manure than other types and grew more abundantly on impoverished soils were deemed by one laborer in Westport 'to be of a soft watery variety which was both unwholesome and unpalatable'.[12]

Poor and monotonous as this food was, matters got worse at certain periods of the year, particularly in Summer – the scarce season. Life became more difficult for women and children, if they were starving, as men rarely begged, particularly at home. Cabbage became a staple food at this time and was often boiled with plain water as the poor could not afford butter or any other dressing except salt and a laborer seldom could obtain milk to consume with his potatoes.[13] If the poor could get a pint of meal, they made gruel of it and poured it over the cabbage. The cabbage dressed in this way was easier to eat and less likely to sicken people. When cabbage was unavailable, people resorted to '*praiseach*' or charlock which grew wild in the corn fields.[14] Eggs were not eaten at this time, as 'they go to the rent or to put a shoe on our foot or a spade in our hand. We sell them now, we used to eat them'.[15] Women mainly foraged when people had to seek alternative food supplies. One man said: 'My wife then goes through the fields and gathers some of the green weeds and boils them'.[16] Others lived principally on herbs gathered in the fields and shellfish from the shore, as well as wild borage from the fields.[17]

---

[12] Appendix A. Evidence of John Doyle, p. 373.
[13] Ibid. Evidence of Thomas O'Hara, p. 365.
[14] Ibid. Evidence of James Brown, p. 366.
[15] Ibid. Evidence of William Butler, p. 198.
[16] Ibid., p. 383.
[17] Ibid. Evidence of Hugh O'Malley, p. 384.

Even when women were able to earn a pittance and were the main breadwinners in a household, they were unable to obtain a sufficiency of food. The case of the Widow Kilboy, who was in this position, and who had paid employment for nine months of the year, describes her food situation as follows:

> 'When earning nothing, persons who are in the habit of employing me have lent me money to be repaid in work when they would have employment for me. At such times we have lived on one meal of dry potatoes in the day. I and my four children have often lived on eight stone of potatoes for the whole week; about sixteen stone would be sufficient for us. We very seldom at any time of the year have milk with our potatoes; we sometimes have a salt herring, but we eat them three times dry for once that we have anything with them and it is not the best even of the potatoes that we have. We have the cheapest and worst sort of lumpers, that we may have them plentiful. I am not able to clothe my children; the wages I can earn are too little even to buy potatoes for them; but the people that employ me and trust me with their property are kind enough to help me now and then with a little meal or seeds beyond my wages'.[18]

It is little wonder then that many women had to beg for food, some at particular seasons of the year; others on a year round basis. Catherine Flynn[19] had begged for eleven of the fifteen years she was married and must beg for most of the year. Many of these women had husbands who were quite unable to support them. In many parishes, such as Kilgeever, the larger proportion of resident beggars 'consisted of the wives and children of *cottiers* or laborers who work occasionally, but are unable to support themselves and families by their holding or labor'.[20]

---

18 Ibid. Evidence of Widow Kilboy, p. 122.
19 Ibid. Evidence of Catherine Flynn, p. 497.
20 Ibid., p. 504.

To make matters worse, laborers who had previously been able to support their wives and families were said 'to have passed their labor at fifty and fifty-five'.[21] The task of supporting them fell to their wives, who often had to beg to do this.

Many women aged seventy and over, particularly if they belonged to the laboring classes, had to resort to begging to get food as many laborers were generally incapable of supporting their aged parents, one half of them being principally supported by what was begged by their wives and children.[22] Widows with young children and the wives of migratory workers often begged to support themselves. Many widows had to beg all year. If a migratory laborer earned sufficient money, his wife could stop begging, at least temporarily, if not she begged all year.

Many only resorted to begging when food supplies ran out and often in a remote part of the country to save face.[23] Particularly when a woman had children, she did better by begging than by staying at home, as a 'woman with a family on the average of years might gather three stone in Winter and one and a half stone in Summer'.[24]

This was a more satisfactory situation than that of many women who would not resort to begging, as some of them felt that they would bring the family into disrepute by so doing. One woman stated:

> 'We often fasted for twenty four hours or lived on one quart of meal or green cabbage boiled without either meal or potatoes. Often one stone of potatoes has been the food of the entire family for two whole days. I never begged, I would rather fast than shame my people that were well-off and decent when times were better, though they are poor today and badly able to help me'.[25]

---

21 Ibid., p. 193.
22 Ibid., p. 194.
23 Ibid., p. 370.
24 Ibid. Rev. Fr. Gibbons, p. 504.
25 Ibid. Evidence of Mary Moran, p. 373.

While it was often stated that women who begged were better off than those who did not, the lot of the woman forced to beg was difficult, despite the generosity of neighbors. It necessitated bringing the family with them in all conditions, as:

'Unless women took their children with them even in the most severe weather, they could not procure them a sufficiency of food; but I have known them to leave them at home, on a single meal, while they themselves went out to beg rather than take them with them in bad clothes in cold wet weather'.[26]

Activities of women to get food during the Famine are dealt with in a special chapter, as is the lot of the wives of migratory laborers.

To realize how drastically the food situation had disimproved, one turns to Arthur Young[27] who, when describing Tirawley in the latter quarter of the previous century, stated that the food of the peasants was potatoes, cockles, herrings and a little meal and where the potatoes are out, oatmeal only. The majority kept cows and those who did not bought milk. Even in Westport, which was much poorer than the Barony of Tirawley, the poor in general lived on potatoes and milk nine months out of twelve, the other three months, bread and milk. All of them had one or two cows. At the time of writing, Young commented that in their domestic economy the men fed the family with their labor in the field and the women paid the rent by spinning. This standard of living was quite impossible in the period under consideration.

A measure of the poverty was the shortage of cooking utensils or lack thereof. Vessels formerly repaired were discarded and this was caused by poverty. 'Many people cannot afford to repair their wooden vessels; once they are damaged, they throw them out on the dunghill and use one pot for everything. Many roast potatoes, not having a pot to boil them'.[28]

---

[26] Ibid., p. 504.
[27] Young, Arthur, *A Tour in Ireland*, Vol. I., p. 246.
[28] Appendix A. Evidence of Brien Deane, Cooper, Kilmore Erris, p. 384.

When people killed animals to relieve famine, many were unable to make the best use of the meat so obtained, either through lack of skill or lack of equipment. In Foxford, in 1847, people were killing horses and salting them as beef. When people killed cows, the most part was left to rot from their inability to cure them.[29]

Once women obtained employment, particularly steady employment, not only did they purchase furniture and clothes but 'above all things diet no longer consisted of merely potatoes'.[30] However, these were in the minority and the struggle to obtain food was, even before the Great Famine, grim and unrelenting. It continued to be so for many people. One cannot but concur with the statement that:

> 'for the laborers of Ireland, food was always the major source of anxiety. Clothing and entertainment were so rudimentary that an acceptable level was fairly easily obtained, not so for the absolute necessities'.[31]

[29] *Mayo Constitution*, January 26, 1847.
[30] Appendix D., p. 24.
[31] Kevin O'Neill, p. 116, *Family and Farm in pre-Famine Ireland* (1984).

Mary Farragher and Jamie O Toole
1840-1927   1834-1924
Married 1864

13. Wedding, 1864. The chair in the picture came from India and is a family heirloom.

4

The Famine

While the Famine with its attendant evils blighted the lives of women all over Ireland, it had a devastating effect on the lives of Mayo women, not only because the Famine affected the County very badly, but because official Famine Relief schemes were very slow to get under way and were quite inadequate over large areas of the County. The poor conditions in housing, food shortages and the incidence of disease were aggravated by the Famine.

Of historical interest are the accounts of the vicissitudes suffered by the people of the County and women's attempts to cope with the Famine and adapt to the changes which it inevitably brought in their lives.

Many eye-witness reports graphically describe the sufferings people endured. The desperate attempts to obtain any kind of food are seen in Erris, where 10,000 people were living or starving on turnips, sand-eels and sea-weed, a diet 'which no-one in England would consider for the meanest animal which he keeps'.[1] There were people in Binghamstown whose only food was bad turnips. Many there had no food at all and were subsisting on the roots of weeds.[2] Deaths from starvation were sometimes reported in newspapers. For instance, the *Galway Vindicator* of June 16th, 1847 recorded the deaths from starvation of Mark Loftus of Killala on June 4th, Mark McDonnell of Ballycastle, January 9th and Matthew Temple of Crossmolina on January 10th, 1847.

Even more horrifying were the stories of privation in the cabins. William Bennett visiting Erris found 'In one cabin a

---

[1] *Transactions*: James H. Tuke. An Account of his visit to Connaught in the Autumn of 1847, p. 205.
[2] Famine Relief Papers. Vol. II. Evidence of W.R. Hamilton. p. 86.

shriveled old woman imploring us to give her something –
baring her limbs partly to show us how the thin flesh hung loose
from her bones – as soon as she attracted our attention. Above
her on something like a ledge was a young woman with sunken
cheeks – a mother I have no doubt – who scarcely raised her
eyes in answer to our enquiries but pressed her hand upon her
forehead with a look of unutterable anguish and despair'.[3]

It was quite some time before food relief schemes were
organized for County Mayo and, as a result, when relief came
it was often too late'.[4] Even when relief was available, several
people were too ill or weak to collect the food so provided.
The Geraghty family was one such: 'The father lying dead and
mother and five children huddled on the floor, all bowed down
by disease, none of the family had been able to go for rations'.[5]
Some felt that the rations were 'a mere enabling the patient to
endure for a little longer time disease and hunger'.[6]

Some women, motivated by a fierce independence and a fear
of the workhouse, tried to stay independent until they collapsed.
In Belmullet, such a woman collapsed in the street. She had not
applied for relief and had 3s. 1d. in her pocket when brought into
the workhouse. Such a sum would have procured food for her, at
least for a time; spending money in this manner, however, would
mean sacrificing her cherished independence.

Among the most desperate were 'widows whose husbands
had recently been taken off by the fever and thus their only
pittance, obtained from the public works, was entirely cut off'.[7]
Many widows, especially those with children, had either to beg

---

3   *Transactions*: Appendix III. An Account of his visit to Erris by Richard D.
    Webb, pp. 163–201.
4   Famine Relief Papers. Board of Works Series 2nd Part. London 1847.
    Volume III. Mr. Ffennell to Mr. Mulvaney. February 23, 1847. p. 157.
5   Famine Ireland I.U.P. Series of British Parliamentary Papers 5th Series.
    Volume II. Evidence of Mr. Hamilton, February 6th, 1848. p. 9.
6   *Transactions*: Letter addressed to the Committee about the condition of
    the different parts of the country, in the Winter of 1846–1847. William
    Edward Forster's Report, p. 154.
7   Famine Relief Papers, 6th Series. 1847–1848. Volume III. Letter of
    W.J. Hamilton, p. 196.

or enter the Workhouses.[8] The Irish Poor Law Relief Act (1 and 2 Vic. c.56 1838) had enacted that no relief should become available outside the workhouses. However, in the desperate circumstances of the time, those hated institutions became filled with widows and children, the aged and weak.[9]

Some slight easing in the conditions for obtaining relief came in 1847, when three Acts were passed among which the principal provisions were as follows: 'Destitute women having two or more legitimate children dependent upon them may be relieved in or out of the Workhouses at the direction of the Guardians'. This provision did nothing for the lot of the unmarried mother, who was generally ostracized by society, but it enabled some widows, at least, to try to retain a grip on their holdings. At times, women claimed widow status to obtain relief to which they were not entitled. Sometimes, these bogus applicants were aided and abetted by conniving landlords who felt that it reduced the onus on them personally to help. An indefatigable investigator of Famine relief claims described one such bogus claim in Kilfian: 'We proceeded next to Mary Reap's house, who would, if she could, persuade us that she was a poor widow, and produced for us a landlord's Certificate No. 500. We found her husband, Michael Quinn, comfortably seated by a roaring fire after returning some hours from his daily labor with the landlord'.[10]

Ironically, some of the food provided, aimed at preventing illness and death, actually helped to cause them. Describing the epidemics in the Westport Union between 1846–1850, Dr. Daly stated that one of the major causes was bad food such as Indian meal supplied to them (relief applicants) which they invariably swallowed after only a few minutes boiling, sometimes cold and raw.[11] Such food seemed to hasten death.

---

8 *Transactions*, Appendix III. Correspondence of Wm. Bennett, pp. 163–201.

9 Trevelyan, C.E. *The Irish Crisis*. London (1848), p. 152.

10 Famine Relief Papers, 6th Series, Vol. 3. Letter of John Palmer, R.O. Kilfian. E.D. to Peter Burrowes, Chairman Ballina Union, p. 200.

11 Appendix to the Final Report of the Commission of Public Works. Famine Relief Papers, Volume 8.

In Ballycroy, poor people died very quickly, if 'they get any strong dose at all (full meal)'.[12] Women's inexperience in culinary matters may have contributed to the number of deaths rather than Indian meal per se. One account stated: 'There is scarcely a woman of the peasant class in the West of Ireland whose culinary skill exceeds the boiling of a potato. Bread is scarcely ever seen and an oven is unknown'.[13] It is interesting to note that in the Castlebar Union, rye-bread was distributed as relief. But Indian meal still continued to be used as relief food and in 1849 the kind of food most commonly in use was 'a mixture of Indian or barley meal with turnips, the latter frequently of the most watery and worst description'.[14]

To obtain the food provided, many women had to work on Famine Relief Schemes, which did not get under way in Mayo until November 1846, despite the fact that the population requiring relief in Mayo consisted of two-thirds of all the people living in Third Class and all who lived in Fourth Class Housing.[15] Far fewer women than men were employed in these schemes and the Barony worst affected by the Famine – Erris – had the least number of people, both men and women, employed in these schemes. On the 7th November 1846, there were 11 men working on Relief Schemes in Erris and four women, while for the County as a whole there was a total of 10,564 able-bodied men and 430 women.[16] By February 6th, 1847, the number of women working on public works had increased from 430 to 2,783 but they were not employed on drainage schemes.[17] The baronies of Clanmorris, Costello, Kilmaine and Murrisk had the least increase in the number of females employed, while the number of women on Relief works had increased ninefold in

---

12 *Transactions*, p. 202.
13 Trevelyan, C.E., op. cit. pp. 7–8.
14 Famine Relief Papers, 6th Series, Volume 3, 1847–48. Evidence of Captain Hamilton, p. 552.
15 Famine Relief Papers, 1847, Vol. VI, p. 1216.
16 Ibid., p. 1216.
17 Famine Relief Papers, Board of Works Series Second Part, London 1847, p. 49.

Gallen and Tirawley and eightfold in Erris. One wonders how far this work helped people, as in Westport it was stated that 'the greatest mortality from fever was among the laborers, both men and women, on the public roads and cold wet boggy hills'.[18]

Many women stayed out of the workhouses and tried to procure food for themselves, while hoping to hold on to their households. This was a vain hope in many instances as many landlords not only availed of the infamous Gregory Clause in the Poor Laws to clear their estates of poor tenants, but flagrantly broke the law to do so – even to the extent of setting fire to beds with occupants in them.[19] One of the most unmerciful landlords in this regard was Mr. John Walsh in Erris, who also took advantage of an occupant's absence to procure food to carry out an eviction.[20] Catherine Hallon returned from the shore to find her roof thrown in (see Addenda). Other landlords effected clearances by refusing, as ex-officio Poor Law Guardians, to recommend their starving tenantry for relief (either as food or employment on the relief schemes) unless they consented to surrender their holdings.

One account shows the effect of the Famine very clearly and reveals the air of complete despair it produced. Deprivation seems, in some instances, to have led to a form of infanticide. Richard D. Webb on a visit of inspection to Erris stated: 'I have heard instances of women willfully neglecting their young children so that they died'. The writer does not blame them. He continues: 'I can wonder at nothing I hear, after what I have seen of their fearful wretchedness and misery'.[21]

There was a sizeable increase in the number of deserted wives, or apparently deserted wives, in at least one Poor Law Union. 'There are a considerable number of deserted women in this Union (Swinford) – women whose husbands are in America

---

[18] Appendix to the Final Report of the Commission of Public Works under the heading: Disease in Ireland. Evidence of Dr. Daly.
[19] Papers Relating to the Relief of Distress and State of Unions in Ireland, pp. 236–237.
[20] Distress Papers: Evidence of Catherine Hallon, p. 237.
[21] *Transactions*: Appendix III. Letter of Richard D. Webb, p. 199.

I BEG to enclose, for the information of the Poor Law Commissioners, a statement showing the periods on which, according to the opinion of the Poor Law Inspectors, the relief to children should stop in their respective Unions.

ENCLOSURE.

STATEMENT showing the date at which the Poor Law Inspectors recommend that the Relief to Children should be closed :—

Unions in which the relief is to be closed on the 20th August.			Unions in which the relief is to be closed on the 31st August.		
No.	Name of Unions.	Number of Children.	No.	Name of Unions.	Number of Children.
1	Ballina,	14,291	1	Boyle,	3,960
2	Belmullet,	3,683	2	Carrick-on-Shannon,	4,140
3	Ballinrobe,	7,023	3	Castlerea,	8,744
4	Ballyshannon,	8,185	4	Kilrush,	4,189
5	Bantry,	9,411	5	Listowel,	7,017
6	Cahirciveen,	2,614	6	Milford,	2,716
7	Castlebar,	4,858	7	Manorhamilton,	4,000
8	Clifden,	4,226	8	Roscommon,	2,117
9	Donegal,	5,955	9	Sligo,	8,000
10	Galway,	4,618	10	Dingle,	2,715
11	Glenties,	6,211			
12	Kenmare,	4,213			47,598
13	Skibbereen,	19,141			
14	Swineford,	19,064			
15	Tuam,	4,640			
16	Westport,	8,380			
		126,513			
		47,598			
	Total number of children,	174,111			

Dublin, 31st July, 1848.   P. E. DE STRZELECKI.

Source: Papers relating to Proceedings for the Relief of the Distress and State of Unions and Workhouses in Ireland, 7th Series – 1848, Miscellaneous, Count Strzelecki to the Poor Law Commissioners.

14. Almost one-third of the children cut off were from Mayo. Within the County, 3 in every 10 came from the Ballina Union, while two fifths came from the Swinford Union. Similar distress is seen in the Skibbereen Union in Cork.

and in England and women not married with several children',[22] which would also incline one to believe that prostitution had become more prevalent. It is noteworthy that this distressed Union had the largest number of children in Mayo dependent

[22] British Parliamentary Papers – Famine Ireland 1847–1848. Volume 3. 6th Series. I.U.P. Letter of Mr. Gibbons to Committee re Swinford Union, March 10, 1848, p. 480.

on Poor Law Relief in July 1848 (33%), followed by the Ballina Union (25%). One can only imagine the consternation when it became known that Poor Law Inspectors recommended that the relief to children should be closed from 20th August 1848 in certain Mayo Unions.

Of the 16 Unions where this assistance was being cancelled, the 6 Mayo Unions contained 45% of the impoverished children. While the stark figures speak for themselves, this action is more understandable, when one learns that each Union in the County was distressed financially at this time.

In the circumstances of the time, many women had to resort to the Workhouses or infirmaries, if they had Famine fever, as fever inspired terror in the general populace. Normally, nursing duties fell to the women but, not always so, especially when they caught fever.[23] The spread of fever was rendered faster by the lack of hygiene, lack of clothing and poor sanitary conditions. Time and again, one reads of fever being caused by the 'want of both day and night covering and insufficient and unwholesome food.[24]

Many areas, such as Kilgeever, had no dispensaries[25] and those stricken by fever might, if they could afford to do so, purchase the care of a nurse-tender. Had dispensaries been available, it is not clear that they would have been availed of. A report from Cong states: 'That the use of the dispensary seems to be at present impeded by the fear that persons connected with it would attempt to interfere with the religious opinions of any patients that might apply for aid',[26] an accusation refuted by the Resident Magistrate. If they became ill, conditions for women both within the workhouses or infirmaries or outside in the hovels were grim. 'In the workhouse at Ballina, the mortality from fever and dysentery has been alarming; but it must be said that a large proportion of the sufferers only apply for admission in the hope that they should be provided with a coffin when

---

[23] Appendix A, p. 291.
[24] Ibid. Evidence of Rev. Mr. Lyons, p. 293.
[25] Ibid., p. 293.
[26] Appendix A. Evidence of Rev. Mr. Waldron, p. 292.

dead, which was more than could be expected if they died outside the workhouse walls'.[27]

There were great differences within the actual infirmaries and workhouses. On November 20, 1847, in Ballinrobe, there was a 'lamentable deficiency in hospital bedding with three fever patients in one bed',[28] while Captain Broughton spoke of conditions in Swinford Workhouse as being 'beautifully clean'.

Even in 1851, there were 7,998 women the workhouses in Mayo by contrast with 4,674 men, but there were fewer women in hospital, 18 women as against 33 men.[29] While we regard these institutions as Draconian, Forbes, referring to the wives of migratory laborers, stated: 'When the mother is enabled to leave the (Westport) Union on the return of her husband, or by any other means, her daughters are often found most anxious to remain in the house'.[30] This, of course, was not allowed by Poor Law regulations.

Fear of fever even prevented the dead from being buried on some occasions. One visitor, calling to a cabin saw 'a father lying near death on one side of the fireplace and on the opposite side of the hut, beneath a ragged quilt, the body of an old woman who had taken shelter and who had died, and as she belonged to nobody there was nobody to bury her'.[31]

In spite of the hardship of the times, the lot of some women improved, if they were lucky enough to be employed, although reservations were expressed about the employment of women on Relief works, especially by medical practitioners. Women fared better on employment schemes set up under private auspices or by charitable organizations during the Famine. Women were sometimes employed on Drainage Schemes by landowners who had received grants under the Land Improvement Act. Colonel Knox-Gore of Ballina, one of the most humane landlords,

---

[27] *Transactions*: Appendix III. Account of Richard D. Webb, p. 198.
[28] I.U.P. Series of British Parliamentary Papers – 4th Series. Famine Volume 2, Ireland 1847–1848. Evidence of Dr. Dempster, p. 56.
[29] British Parliamentary Papers, Census 1851. Volume VIV, Table XI.
[30] Forbes, John. *Memorandums*, p. 278.
[31] *Transactions*: Appendix III. Account of Richard D. Webb, p. 201.

15. Burrishoole Abbey.

took £2,500 under the Land Improvement Act and employed between one and two hundred men and women in carrying out improvements under this Act.[32] In Newport, the good done by the employment supplied by the flax works 'manifested itself in the comfortable appearance of the work people, both men and women, when compared with the wretchedness of those not fortunate enough to be employed by them'.[33]

---

[32] Famine, Volume 4, 8th Series, 1849. Statement by Col. Arthur Knox-Gore to Mr. Famly, p. 9.

[33] *Transactions*: Appendix XXX. Extract from a Report from Arthur Barrington, 14th July, 1849, p. 434.

Some employment schemes were funded by Relief organizations, such as The Society of Friends, which provided both short-term relief and training in skills. These organizations realized that the long-term solution to the misery of the women's lives lay in providing them with skills and worthwhile employment. For instance, The Belfast Ladies Industrial Association for Connaught (in association with the Society of Friends) aimed to qualify 'young females of Connaught to become independent members of society through their own industry: they sent fifty four teachers of approved qualifications to poor females who formerly earned nothing. They paid wages to the amount of £5,000 a year which was later raised to £7,500'.[34] This aid was aimed at the most indigent section of society as with few exceptions all the girls were of the poorest class. 'Fifteen pupils in one school have been common beggars. Of 63 girls in one school, 42 are orphans and of 83 in another, only 13 have both parents living'.[35] These girls were working in knitting and the sewing of muslin. That these girls could achieve high standards of excellence is shown by the fact that their work occupied an honorable place at the Great Exhibition and commanded the highest prices in the Scotch and English markets.[36] Had employment been available on a sufficiently large scale, many deaths caused by starvation and disease could have been avoided, as women would have had money available to purchase ample food supplies, despite the failure of the potato crop.

Of great interest are the accounts of aid rendered by women during the Famine. Many women took an active part in food distribution and in providing the destitute with clothing. Many of these ladies were either members of landlords' families or members of the Church of Ireland, as well as smaller numbers from other religious sects. Many helped to administer relief supplied by the Society of Friends. While occasional accusations

---

[34] Society of Friends, Appendix XXXI. Statement from letters of Dr. Edgar of Belfast. p. 438.

[35] Ibid. Appendix XXXI, p. 438.

[36] Ibid., p. 438.

of proselytism were made against some in a position to distribute meal or other relief, in general one must concur with the statement that 'Quakers knew that in an area like Erris, the parson, his wife and his daughters, or anyone who manned a soup kitchen in 'Black '47' had barely enough strength to serve the physical needs of the people, let alone time to engage in proselytizing'.[37] The Quakers were scrupulous with regard to checking the credentials of those whom they appointed to administer relief, and they themselves have never been accused of any attempts at proselytism. In spite of their care, however, murmurs of protest arose which, on occasions, led to much acrimonious publicity. Such was the affair of Catherine Plunket, a relative of the militant evangelical Protestant Archbishop of Tuam, Thomas Plunket, who owned an estate at Tourmakeady. Here, he established a school run by Catherine. The Quakers had given her funds for distribution in the area, as she was one of the few resident members of the gentry. Tales about her encouragement of proselytism soon abounded in the Lough Mask area.[38] Yet, this episode, the cause of much dissension, should not blind one to the Herculean work done for Famine relief by other members of her Church.

Erris at this time was the 'fag end of misery'.[39] The Rector of Kilcommon, Rev. Samuel Stock, had lived in the Belmullet area since 1816. He was the chief organizer of famine relief administration in the area and he worked closely with the parish priests. Often he assisted his wife and daughters to man a soup kitchen. This good lady, Mrs. Stock, not only manned the chief soup kitchen in Belmullet in the kitchen of the Rectory, but she also set up a 'clothing manufactory' for industrious women in the Belmullet area until fever disrupted the venture. On Clothing Application No. 2517, dated 1848, from Mrs. Stock to the Quakers, is appended a note commending the Stocks for being 'active parties' in relief.[40]

---

[37] Bowen, D. *Souperism, Myth or Reality*, p. 124.
[38] Ibid., p. 158.
[39] Nicholson, Asenath. *Lights and Shades*, p. 295.
[40] Bowen, D., op. cit. pp. 190–192.

At Doonfeeney, the established Church parson was Francis Little, who worked closely with the local parish priest, Rev. Martin Hart. The *Tirawley Herald* of 20th March 1848 reported the death of his wife, June, from Famine fever 'caught in the discharge of a charitable duty which she was always foremost in performing'.

In Crossmolina Parish, the Protestant Curate was Henry St. George Caulfield Knox, who had married the daughter of his parson, Richard St. George. A visitor to the parish in 1847 found Mrs. St. George making soup, but 'no one else appeared to be doing anything in the place which contains 2,000 inhabitants, one half of whom are in a state of desperate want'.[41] This lady also acted as an amateur physician and looked after a multitude of abandoned or orphaned children.

Help provided by Church of Ireland parsons, ably assisted by the female members of their families, was particularly important in the Kilfian area, where the local landlord, Sir Roger Palmer, was notorious for his refusal to pay rates, or to assist in the formation of a local relief Committee. St. George Knox, the local Parson, said in his Application to the Society of Friends (No.18, January 13th, 1847) for Kilfian Parish: 'Hundreds would already have died, if it were not for the relief I was able to afford them'. His wife, Mrs. Fannie Knox, spent £200 a month from her own resources to feed three hundred families plus another three hundred beggars daily at her family home, Fahy, in Kilfian Parish. She also helped her mother in directing operations at the soup boilers. These two ladies also organized a weaving and spinning establishment for the poor of the town.[42] The Catholic Vicar General ably expressed the feelings of the destitute people of this parish, when he wrote to the Quakers praising the work of the Protestant clergy and their wives, while he condemned Sir Roger Palmer and the other absentee landlords.[43]

The *Tyrawley Herald* of December 30th, 1847 printed a letter from George Read, the Protestant Curate in Ballina. Once

[41] Simms, W.D., *Narrative.*
[42] Bowen, D., op. cit. p. 204.
[43] Quaker Relief Application 188, February 1847.

16. Achill Island. The Settlement at Dugort.

again, we read of an able wife helping her parson husband. He wrote: 'Late and early my house was beset by starving creatures, clamoring for food. My servants were all engaged in helping them. My wife and myself had offered to take their place, when they were fatigued'.

Ladies of various religious persuasions took part in the distribution of clothing, but not to the same extent as in the distribution of food. Indeed, there were complaints that there were not enough people to work in this area. In Ballina, Rev. Thomas Armstrong said he knew of no one who would help him in the distribution of clothes.[44]

44 Ibid. Clothing, 29th February, 1847.

Some difficulties with regard to getting people to distribute food and clothing in an area such as Ballina may have been caused by the arguments and dissensions which prevailed among various religious groups in the town at this time, where tempers were frayed by shortages, overwork and despair. Accusations of partiality in the distribution of clothing were made, as is clear from the application made by Theresa Armstrong, wife of the Presbyterian Minister Thomas Armstrong who wrote asking for Quaker help, saying she wished to work 'singly' in helping the poor, wishing to keep free from any imputation of sectarianism or favoritism with which others in this town (Ballina) are charged.[45]

Areas, which did not have a parson or other active gentleman, suffered greatly by their absence. They also missed the female members of their families who usually organized the day-to-day running of these institutions, such as Soup Kitchens, often set up by Clergy and gentry. A Quaker visitor, Edmund Richards, noted what happened in the Mullet peninsula when there was nobody, such as Mrs. Knox, to take charge. The ship 'Scourge' on which Mr. Richards came to Erris put off two boilers at Killybegs in the Mullet; there was no one available locally to set up a food station and the boiler was not operated and the people died.[46]

One cannot but concur with the following comments about the parsons and their wives: 'He (the parson) was a boon and a blessing to the parish in which he was located. His wife was generally the Lady Bountiful, to whom the peasant applied in all ailments with a certainty of obtaining gratuitous relief – the nearest dispensary being perhaps a dozen miles off'.[47]

The help rendered by these ladies was particularly helpful as there were no Catholic female religious orders in Mayo until the last years of the period under consideration. The Sisters of Mercy, who came to Ballina on the invitation of Fr. Maloney, began to relieve the needs of the poor and fill a great social need.[48]

---

[45] Ibid., p. 71, 29th April 1847.
[46] *Transactions*, p. 172.
[47] Hall, S.C. *Retrospect of a Long Life*, p. 347.
[48] Mercy Convent Ballina Records.

S.P. 1518: THE MISSION SETTLEMENT, DUGORT, ACHILL ISLAND.

The Achill Mission Society was an evangelising body introduced to the island in 1834 by the Reverend Edward Nangle. It was based at Dugort and established a church, schools, modern houses, and a printing press for the publication of religious texts. In 1851 by means of subscriptions from England and Ireland it purchased a large estate from the local landlord, Sir Richard O'Donnel. The tenants on the estate paid rents much as before but now the Mission and its trustees were in effect the landlord.

The Mission was responsible for a general raising of the standard of living on the island through education and the introduction of modern farming methods. Its evangelical aim met with considerable success, and a member of the committee wrote in 1886: 'It must not be forgotten that since the Missionary work was commenced, more than 1,000 persons have emigrated from the island and neighbourhood who were converts from Romanism.'

The map below is from the Ordnance Survey, 25 inch scale, Mayo sheet XLII.12, surveyed 1897.

17. The mission settlement, Dugort, Achill Island (Map).

All the help given by women was gladly given. The cost was great, not only in material terms, but also in terms of human suffering and in some cases death, occasioned by contact with the destitute. Many of these who received help had a low form of infection called 'road fever' to which the poor had built up some immunity, but which killed many better off people, such as Mrs. Little.

While some instances of kindness and help rendered have been recorded, one cannot doubt that women who were in a position to do so gave all the help they could, in the tragic circumstances of the time. These tragic circumstances were aggravated by the beliefs that the Irish were 'a feckless people' and the Famine was 'The Visitation of God'. Official responses to the Famine by government were rather tardy. There were widespread prejudices against providing relief free of charge and fears that large sections of the populace would become dependants in institutions, such as Workhouses. It was also felt that the cultural failings of the Irish were an important causative factor of the Great Famine, an idea which resonates at the present time. A modern food writer and historian, Armstrong, argues that 'as personal flaws recur, so too can cultural failings be identified in communities across distances in time' in an article entitled 'Blight of boom and burst is of our own making' (*The Sunday Times*, 4th January, 2015), argues that the Famine and the crash of Celtic Tiger Ireland were fed by a failure to recognize cultural flaws. He sees parallels between the huge population growth in population in pre-Famine Ireland as a reaction to the seemingly unlimited supply of potatoes and the response of the Irish nation to the rise in property values during the Celtic Tiger era; 'Both suggest a lack of restraint and a failure to acknowledge clear warning signs. In both, the trauma of colonization is evident'. He refers to the habit of apportioning blame: in modern Ireland, bankers and profiteers have been excoriated, while during the Famine 'the cupidity … avariciousness of merchants, tradesmen etc., were wringing fortunes … out of the vitals of the poor and reaping a golden harvest to the shameful open plunder of the public' to quote from the article 'Must the People Starve' published in *The Galway Vindicator* in December 1846. Armstrong is not alone in lamenting the failure to acknowledge that delusional greed was a major component of several levels of society in both eras.

Less obvious are some specific health problems, found in certain sections of the population, notable mainly in the West of Ireland and in many descendants of Irish Famine emigrants, which can be attributed to a large extent to the effects of genetic mutations in response to Famine conditions. Developments in the field of Epigenetics (literally 'around the gene') have advanced the study of Haemochromatosis (Hemochromatosis), an autosomal recessive disorder which can be passed to a child from both parents. This has led to the study of how the Great Famine altered the genes of children born decades later. The new field of Historic Genomics has made the investigation of genetic mutation over periods of time possible. The HFE gene mutation is central to the study of Haemochromatosis, which originated in Europe with a Celtic or Viking migrant ancestor. Famine and a very poor diet contributed to a mutation of genes to absorb extra iron. In Ireland, the effects of the 'life destroying absence of adequate nutrition' were exacerbated by the consumption of huge amounts of tea. Those without this gene would have died in disproportionately large numbers during the Famine. Tracey Mary Halloran in *The Western People* of March 27th, 2015 in an article entitled 'Me and My Celtic Gene – Haemochromatosis Lives in the West of Ireland' cites the work of Dr Thos. P. Duffy of the Yale University School of Medicine who posed the research question why certain people survived the Famine.His research strongly suggests that the answer probably lay in the gene pool. In an article 'The Great Hunger and the Celtic Gene' published in *Irish America*, August/September 2013, he argues that in famine times, the essential factors in iron delivery to the system are reduced in malnourished individuals. This negative iron balance was made worse by the large consumption of tea which adversely affects the absorption of iron. The Great Famine magnified the importance of the HFE gene for Haemochromatosis. In an ironic twist of fate, the mutation that can fatally exaggerate iron accumulation in normal times made the critical difference of maintaining iron balance in many individuals during the famine ensuring their survival.

Despite the emigration of many Famine survivors to the USA and Australia bringing Haemochromatosis (sometimes called the Celtic Curse) with them, a notable number of those with the Celtic Gene for this disease remained in Ireland with Mayo having a high concentration. It is no exaggeration to state that in matters of health, as well as in other fields, the Famine has cast a long, dark shadow on the lives of Famine survivors and very many of their descendants.

5

Employment

An eminent historian has written that 'the social and economic condition of the bulk of the population of Ireland in the decades preceding the Famine had reached the nadir',[1] shown in the decreased opportunities for women. There were many causes for this situation, including the decline in prices for agricultural produce coupled with high rents, the collapse of the weaving and linen industries after 1815, reduced demand for textiles and lower prices for some textile products, such as stockings.

Before the Industrial Revolution, there was much cottage industry in Great Britain and Ireland. While in England, many women moved from the home to the factory, this did not happen in Ireland, with the exception of the North East. The Famine delivered a final crippling blow to domestic industry. Whereas the weaving industry had failed earlier, now the spinning of wool, cotton and linen failed causing a dramatic drop in the numbers of women employed between 1841 and 1851. In fact, the main source of independent income enjoyed by women all but vanished.[2] Women made frantic efforts in an effort to keep an independent income and thus one notices a great increase in the number of women huxtering, curing fish, etc., in an attempt to earn income.

To compound the misfortune of reduced employment opportunities in textiles, the changed pattern of agriculture brought about by the Famine also led to reduced employment opportunities for women, as livestock farming was less labor

---

[1]   O'Neill, T.P. 'The Great Irish Famine, 1845–1852' in *Irish Ecclesiastical Record*, Vol. LXIX, November 1947.

[2]   Lee, Joseph J., 'Women and the Church since the Famine' in *Women in Irish Society: the historical dimension*, p. 37.

intensive than tillage farming, which had been more common before the Famine. In general, the only increased opportunity for employment between the years 1841 and 1851 was by becoming a servant, with an increase of 0.4% being noted in female servants and 1.6% in the case of male servants.[3]

The Famine weakened the position of women in Irish society. 'Before the Famine women's economic contribution was so essential to the family that they enjoyed economic independence'.[4] Women's reduced earning power probably tilted the balance of economic power within the family in the male direction. This economic change which affected a woman's independence and standard of living was a relevant factor in the declining marriage rate after the Famine.

During this period, there were few opportunities for employment for women outside the home. There were some jobs in agriculture, many of them seasonal and poorly paid, which were often given to men in preference to women workers. Dean Lyons stressed that 'since the linen manufacture ceased, the women have nothing to do but collect manure (probably seaweed) and attend to the land'.[5] The extra numbers of girls seeking employment in agriculture also meant that unscrupulous employers could exploit them and use their desperation to pay them less than the going rate for such work.

The number of women workers potentially employable in agriculture was limited by the number of people who could afford to pay hired help and, as servants were fed by the employer at the time, paid help were often let go when food supplies, particularly the potato, became scarce. In some areas, there seem to have been more jobs for young girls or women in agriculture than for more mature ladies. In several areas,[6] women were rarely employed except in their own business. As unmarried ladies were still called 'girls' when they had reached old age, this description may have applied mainly to married women.

---

3   Table XX, General Report, 1851 Census.
4   Lee, op. cit., p. 37.
5   Devon Commission, Part I, Chapter XIII, p. 515.
6   Appendix D, H.C. Parliamentary Papers, Vol. XXXI, p. 28.

All through the County, some girls were employed on a seasonal basis on all types of farming tasks. 'Girls are commonly hired by the more comfortable farmers for a single quarter on some occasion of hurry and sent back to their families when potatoes become dear and their support expensive'.[7] Their work was generally in demand in harvest and Spring, the 'throng seasons'.[8] In Autumn, they were employed in digging potatoes.[9] In the Castlebar area, they were sometimes employed to bind the sheaves of oats when reaping,[10] and also when saving hay.[11]

In general, women were not employed for such work, if men were available;[12] in Ballinrobe 'only the poor would employ the women and children at planting potatoes or picking them'.[13] When employed, women received lower wages than men for the same work. Women in occasional agricultural employment usually earned about 2*d*. a day,[14] although at Cong women received 3*d*. or 4*d*. according to strength or age.[15] It was stated that 'stout women' got the same rate as men.[16] How did one define a stout woman? Perhaps the term applied to a known hearty worker rather than a lady with a fuller figure.

One notes desperate attempts made by women to try to find sources of independent income. Of necessity, these involved employment which did not require much cash or expertise to set up. More women took to huxtering and dealing in eggs. The latter seemed to be popular with widows. Ironically, the depression in agriculture which caused farmers to sell eggs, which had been used as food in more prosperous times, helped to boost this trading in eggs, which was hard earned income. One cannot but admire the resilient spirit that motivated a woman,

---

7   Appendix A, Evidence of Mr. Jack Doyle, p. 373.
8   Appendix D, p. 27.
9   Ibid. Evidence of Rev. M. Conway, p. 29.
10 Ibid. Evidence of Lt. Col. James M'Alpine, p. 19.
11 H.C. Parliamentary Papers, Vol. XXVI (1837–1838).
12 Appendix D, p. 19.
13 Supplement to Appendix D. Evidence of Courtney Kenny, p. 24.
14 Appendix D, p. 20.
15 Ibid., p. 19, also p. 25.
16 Ibid., p. 25.

such as the wife of Thomas Burke of Cong. 'She goes into the far part of Connemara to get the eggs, she carries a bit of bread with her or some potatoes to boil on the way, or gets a part of the meal at any house she calls at; she takes her eggs to the market of Tuam and after travelling sixty miles one way and sixty miles the other she is glad to have 2*s*. 6*d*. profit at home'.[17] Others resorted to various forms of trading, such as selling fruit.[18]

One group of women who found it very difficult to find jobs in agriculture were widows, particularly those with young children. Many who might employ a woman were loath to employ one with young children, as they would also have to feed the children and, unless motivated by charity, employers tried to employ single girls.

Widows also found it very difficult to obtain employment in the textile industry, yet it was stated that they lived lives of 'virtuous poverty'[19] and made great efforts to provide for themselves. It was stated that a 'widow is never known to beg if she can maintain herself by her industry'.[20] This struggle to earn a living became more difficult during this period because of the decline in almost every aspect of the textile industry on which so many relied. Even those who received some little employment received very poor payment for their efforts. One widow received 6*d*. a week spinning and paid 5*d*. a week for the cabin she lived in. Others worked for 2*d*. a day and their food.[21] Some knitted, a most unrewarding task. Half a pound of wool might be manufactured into three or four pairs of thin socks, which commonly sold at 3*d*. or 3½*d*. each.[22] Another witness stated: 'Nothing can be made by knitting, unless they mix with the woolen yarn tow, or the short wool of the tuck mill – which could only be procured by interest with the miller'.[23]

[17] Appendix A. Evidence of Thomas Burke, p. 501.
[18] Ibid., p. 12.
[19] Ibid., p. 120.
[20] Appendix A, p. 123.
[21] Ibid., p. 124.
[22] Ibid., p. 124.
[23] Ibid., p. 124.

18. The Village of Dooagh, Achill Island consisting of one storey houses with thatched roofs using the tradtitional *Scolbs* to fasten the thatch.

Few laborers' widows were able to support themselves by their industry and then 'in the most laborious and wretched manner'.[24] Many were reduced to begging. Those begging were often better off than those who attempted to earn their living.

From a material point of view, women such as the Widow Kilboy in Ballina would have had an easier life, if she begged.

---

[24] Ibid., p. 122.

She was employed in kiln-drying oats and was obliged for this purpose to watch the kiln, without intermission, for twenty four hours for which she earned from 7*d.* to 4*d.* for each kiln cast. At one time, she had been three weeks without lying on a bed, not sleeping. At most her wages were 2*s.* 6*d.* She was employed for about 9 months of the year. In spite of all these efforts, she was often distressed, particularly in Summer. 'I am sure most of the beggars live better than we'.[25] One feels that widows who resorted to trading, perhaps in delph at fairs and markets or huxtering eggs, fish or fruit achieved as much with far less effort.

A very popular means of livelihood was that of selling or making *poteen*, (illicit or bootleg whiskey) regarded as the most profitable employment a widow, or 'industrious woman', could engage in; it provided a very poor living, if one judges by appearances. One lady dealing in the product is described as 'all but naked and had no other clothes but what she stood up in'.[26] Many people traded in *poteen*, despite the fact that convictions for the sale of this product were harshly dealt with in the Courts. 'Parliament' whiskey was expensive and had a high rate of excise duty, which boosted the demand for *poteen*. (The type of work undertaken by women was frequently determined by the initial cost of setting oneself up in trading and the cash available to them, in a cash-starved economy). However, it was one of the few trades for which one needed little initial cash, unlike weaving which was relatively costly to set up. 'There,' exclaimed one widow, pointing to a whiskey bottle, 'is my sole dependence. I have no means on earth to keep my children inside the door with me, but to borrow 1*s.* from one neighbor or other to buy a drop of poteen to sell again'.[27]

The 1841 Census records that the employment of women in agriculture was limited to certain positions. No women were employed as ploughmen, gardeners, graziers, land agents, land stewards, gamekeepers, malsters or brewsters. Fifteen women only were classified as farmers but 6,215 women were employed

[25] Ibid., p. 122.
[26] Ibid., p. 122.
[27] Ibid., p. 122.

as laborers in that year. There were 67 female herds over 15 and 234 under 15 employed in that year.[28]

By 1851, some changes had taken place in the employment of women in agriculture. In this year, there were 7,219 women employed as farmers, laborers and servants. In 1851, 38 female herds over 15 and 113 under 15 were employed. Thus, there was a decline of 121 in the numbers of herds under 15 in a ten year period. This reflects the steep decline in the numbers of domestic animals which occurred during the Famine years.

Several factors accounted for the increased number of women egg dealers. The decline in prices for agricultural products meant that people had to sell eggs to clothe their children or provide themselves with tools at a time when there was increased demand for eggs in the English market. Women needed little cash to begin dealing in eggs. Many women probably used eggs produced by their own hens to set them up in business. Thus, the number of egg dealers increased by 100% between 1841 and 1851. The 1851 Census shows that a growth in the market for fowl had developed in the meantime. It was one of the most reliable ways for women to earn an independent income and was an entirely female occupation. Huxters and provision dealers were mainly female, with three times as many so employed in 1851 as there had been in 1841. Even more dramatic was the increase in the number of female fishmongers from fourteen in 1841 to 108 in 1851. The fishing industry along the west coast was much better organized in the intervening years, chiefly aided by capital supplied by the Society of Friends. The art of fish curing had been taught as well. No female fish curer was listed in 1841 with nine women so employed in 1851. Thus dealing in eggs, provisions, fish, became an important source of income for women in these years.

More women began to be employed in dairying as dairy keepers and milk dealers. In 1841, 3 times as many were employed as dairy keepers (milk dealing was not mentioned in 1841 Census) as dairy keepers in 1851 and milk dealers in 1851.

---

[28] Table VI, 1841 Census British Parliamentary Papers.

While employment for women in particular areas of agricultural employment remained static, there was growth in other sectors. The position of female miller was static, with an equal number of female bakers in 1841 and 1851. Women comprised a quarter of the people employed in this industry.

There was a slight increase in the number of female confectioners. In spite of the Famine, there were still enough people wealthy enough to provide employment for this number of confectioners. But this industry seemed to be static, if not in actual decline, as there was only one learner under the age of 15.

The position of water carrier disappeared between 1841 and 1851. I have not been able to find a satisfactory explanation for this. The increases in some categories of agricultural employment did not balance the losses in female employment in other sections; however, the picture in this industry was far more cheerful than that which pertained to the textile industry, which was that of unrelieved gloom.

In 1841, women carders numbered 442, with 52 under the age of 15. By 1851, this number had been reduced to 84. The number of women spinning flax in 1841 was 8,839, a number which was almost quartered in 1851. Almost as drastic was the reduction in the numbers of spinners of wool: 6,641 adult females in 1841 and 372 under the age of 15. By the year 1851, the total number of females in this employment was reduced to 1,688. Even more drastic was the reduction in the number of women employed under the heading unspecified textiles, from 13,766 in 1841 to 1,030 in 1851. The numbers of winders was reduced from 66 to 29. The only increase in female employment in this section was in flax dressing, which had 82 extra women employed in 1851, with a total employment of 135.

The reduced numbers of carders and spinners merely reflect the depressed prices for knitted articles and the destruction of the Irish weaving industry, in the face of machine made items of clothing from England and the cash famine which did not allow the Irish people to buy woven garments.

The story of weaving in this period is very interesting. A knowledge of weaving among women was widespread in

a predominantly male occupation. The industry decline is reflected in towns such as Ballina where, as early as 1835, very many cabins which had formerly been occupied by weavers had become vacant, because they could no longer pay the rent. A residual knowledge of the art of weaving remained, though it is not reflected in the employment figures in this period.

In 1841, just 4 women were employed in weaving woolen goods and 188 men. There were 108 women in unspecified weaving and 2,684 men. These figures do not tell the whole story as weaving provided much temporary employment for women during the Famine. Many relief schemes providing employment were based on their skills in weaving and knitting. While many of these schemes did not outlive the Famine and could be regarded as economic failures, they were of outstanding social value and by providing employment for women, they provided them with the means to keep them and their families alive.

Many individuals set up schemes employing women as weavers. Mrs. Stock, wife of the Protestant Rector of Kilcommon, set up a 'clothing manufactory' in Belmullet, which continued until fever disrupted the work.[29] Mrs. Knox as part of her Famine relief work, set up a weaving and spinning establishment for the poor of Kilfian.[30] The wife of Rev. J. Knox, Gildea organized a scheme of weaving in the Newport area in 1847 which employed between 500–600 women outworkers as linen weavers.[31] Some of the schools set up by religious groups, such as the Presbyterian school in Ballina, taught weaving and sewed muslin work.[32] Much money distributed by the Central Relief Committee was used to set up employment in weaving linen. They funded flax operations in Newport and Ballina.[33] The linen weaving industry led to downstream employment for women in the flax industry. In the Newport area, Sir Richard O'Donnell had received

---

[29] Nicholson, Asenath, *Light and Shades*, p. 295.
[30] Bowen, D., *Souperism, Myth or Reality*, p. 204.
[31] Trevelyan, C.E., *The Irish Crisis*, p. 131.
[32] Forbes, J., *Memorandums*, p. 17.
[33] Society of Friends, *Transactions*, p. 434.

money from the Society of Friends and later had received much flax seed. He employed 1,000 laborers chiefly women to harvest flax.[34]

Migration also affected the weaving industry. As times became more difficult, many migratory workers brought home second-hand woolen or cotton clothing with them from Scotland and England. The troggers brought linen with them from Northern Ireland to Scotland and bought second-hand woolen goods with the proceeds. They returned to Ireland and peddled these goods. Of course, this further depressed an already depressed weaving industry. This trend continued and knowledge of weaving declined over much of the County. This continued even after the period under discussion and is reflected in the situation in Foxford on the arrival of the Sisters of Charity. It was said: 'The art of spinning and weaving wool, which still maintained itself in districts further West had died out here; shoddy and rags had taken the place of the home-spun flannel with which the peasant of Connemara still clothed himself'.[35] Thus by 1851, weaving employed very few women.

There was a huge drop in the number of seamstresses employed, reflecting the decline in the textile industry in general. In the year 1841, 8,402 women had been employed as seamstresses with 50 by 1851. The decline in the number of dressmakers, however, was not so drastic. 898 had been employed in 1841 and 738 in 1851, a decrease of 160. The number of milliners dropped by almost half from 84 to 45. It seemed necessary to employ dressmakers to make or mend clothing, but the economic climate of the time and the general aura of depression did not favor feminine fripperies, and women could more easily do with an old hat than an old gown. Knitting was not as badly affected as some other sections of the textile trade. 1,883 had been employed as knitters in 1841, 1,511 in 1851. With the decline in the prices of wool in the late forties, perhaps more people were able to afford wool to knit small garments, such as coarse socks.

---

[34] Tuke, James H., *Visit to Connaught*, p. 6.
[35] Finlay, T.A., *Foxford and the Providence Woollen Mills* (Booklet, Dublin).

The whole question of work for servants is of great social interest. In 1841,[36] one learns that 3.3% of males in the County were employed as servants and 4.3% of females. At this time, there were more male servants in every parish; in the Barony of Tirawley where they out numbered female servants 4 to 1. The situation in 1851 is not as clear, because data for the Census was analyzed under different headings. Under one heading, we find Farmers' Laborers and Servants numbered 7,219 with 1,603 under the age of 15. There were 5,043 ladies employed as domestic servants and 729 under the age of 15. However, in practice, domestic servants were very frequently sent to labor in the fields.[37] The number of male farmers' servants and laborers had been almost halved between 1841 and 1851, with a less spectacular decrease in the number of employed male farm laborers under the age of 15. The situation which obtained with regard to the employment of women as farm laborers and servants was not so clear. There was an increase in the category of female laborers over 15, from 6,215 in 1841 to 7,318 in 1851, an increase of 1,004. As well, many domestic servants also had to work on agricultural tasks, especially in the 'throng seasons'. There was a decline, however, in the number of girls under 15, who were employed as farm laborers from 1,777 in 1841 to 1,603 in 1851, a decrease of 174.

Baronies such as Tirawley, Costello and Carra employed the largest number of servants. In Tirawley, most female servants were employed in towns, sometimes outnumbering male servants. Crossmolina town had 48 female servants and 20 male. This pattern was not generally repeated in rural areas. While the number of female servants outnumbered male servants by 2 to 1 in Crossmolina town, this situation was reversed in the Crossmolina rural area, where 210 male servants and 134 female servants were employed. In Kilbride, as in Kilfian there were twice as many female servants.

Both the more prosperous and very poor parishes employed an almost equal number of male and female servants. Such was

---

[36] Table I, 1841 Census, p. 400.
[37] Appendix D. Evidence of John Fausset, p. 29.

the position in Ballysakeery, which was relatively prosperous and in Lacken, which was very poor and which employed 49 female and 67 male servants. Rathreagh, also poor, employed nineteen female and 15 male servants.

Some women were lodging house keepers in 1851. This post was popular with widows. If they had a house and furniture, they tried to support themselves by opening feeding houses and letting beds[38] particularly in larger towns. There were 7 such in Kilrnaine[39] who earned 2d. by letting a bed for the night to travelers, or who charged 6d. to 8d. for a poor family for the night. It was only a fairly well off woman who had a house and furniture who could earn her living in this way. It was strictly an urban occupation as in the country, it was usual for poor travelers to obtain lodgings free; such wandering travelers looked for a house with a good rick of turf so as to be sure of comfortable, warm, free lodgings. There were 2 male Hotel and Inn Keepers listed in 1851.

By 1851, women had obtained some posts in the medical field. There were 22 midwives and 1 bathkeeeper. The 45 registered nurse tenders were sometimes employed by people with surplus cash, if a family was stricken by fever or other illness. By a savage irony, the Famine which wrecked the livelihoods of so many women also created some employment opportunities. The post of wardmaid was developed in the Temporary Fever Hospitals. In June 1847, Ballina Temporary Hospital had 2 nurses and 1 wardmaid, Kilmaine, 2 wardmaids and 4 nurses, Westport had two nurses and 1 wardmaid in July of the same year, and Ballinrobe Temporary Hospital had 2 nurses and 2 wardmaids.[40] This new position did not disappear after the Famine. There was a dire need for trained medical personnel. Many midwives were quacks. Dean Lyons, on being questioned, stated that no midwife in his large parish of Kilmore Erris was trained. He recounted with horror the story of a 'peasant within the Mullet who took it upon himself to be an accoucheur and killed several

---

[38] Appendix A, p. 120.
[39] Supplement to Appendix E, p. 26.
[40] Famine Relief Papers, Board of Works Series, Vol. 8, 1846–1853.

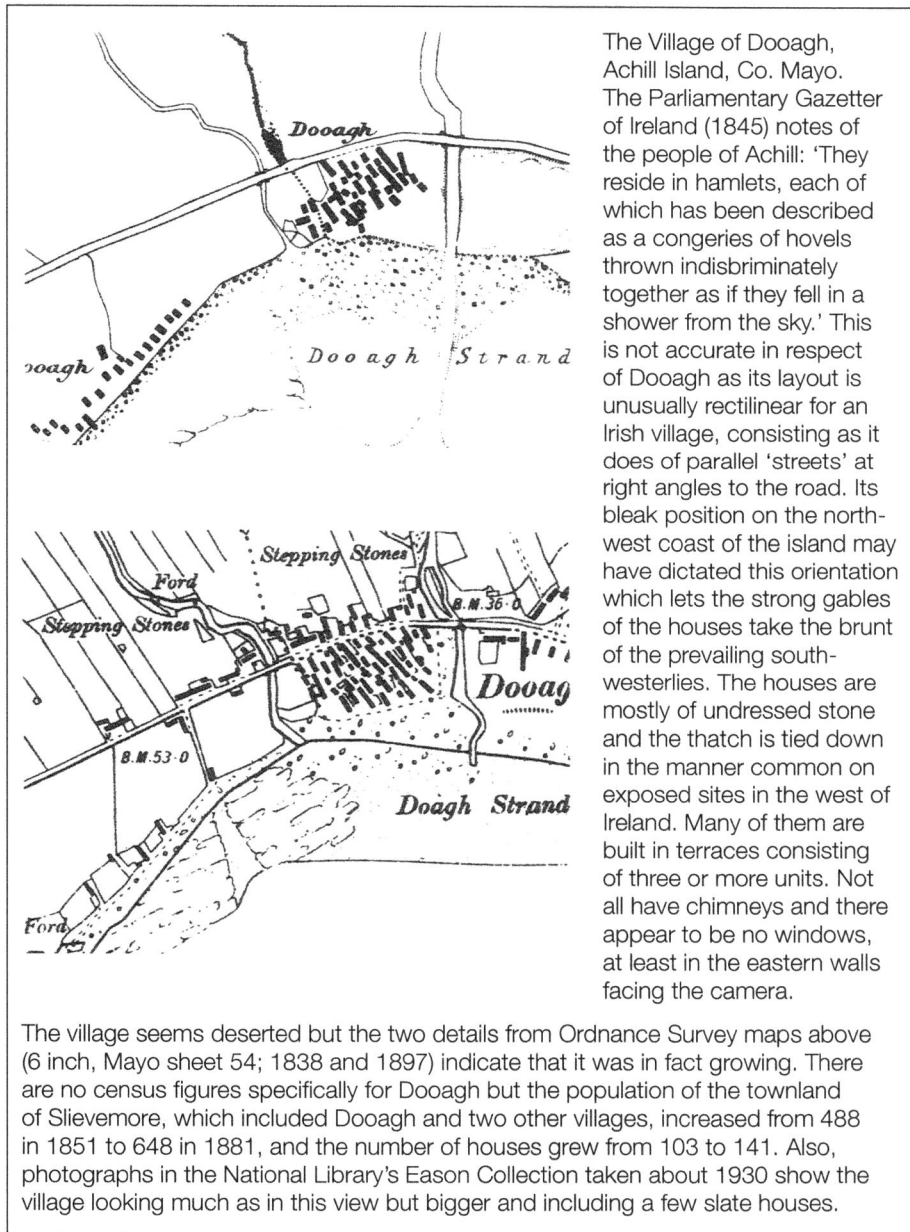

The Village of Dooagh, Achill Island, Co. Mayo. The Parliamentary Gazetter of Ireland (1845) notes of the people of Achill: 'They reside in hamlets, each of which has been described as a congeries of hovels thrown indisbriminately together as if they fell in a shower from the sky.' This is not accurate in respect of Dooagh as its layout is unusually rectilinear for an Irish village, consisting as it does of parallel 'streets' at right angles to the road. Its bleak position on the north-west coast of the island may have dictated this orientation which lets the strong gables of the houses take the brunt of the prevailing south-westerlies. The houses are mostly of undressed stone and the thatch is tied down in the manner common on exposed sites in the west of Ireland. Many of them are built in terraces consisting of three or more units. Not all have chimneys and there appear to be no windows, at least in the eastern walls facing the camera.

The village seems deserted but the two details from Ordnance Survey maps above (6 inch, Mayo sheet 54; 1838 and 1897) indicate that it was in fact growing. There are no census figures specifically for Dooagh but the population of the townland of Slievemore, which included Dooagh and two other villages, increased from 488 in 1851 to 648 in 1881, and the number of houses grew from 103 to 141. Also, photographs in the National Library's Eason Collection taken about 1930 show the village looking much as in this view but bigger and including a few slate houses.

19. The Village of Dooagh, Achill Island. Layout and explanatory note.

women and children. He was tried twice for it but acquitted on both occasions for want of legal evidence'.[41] Medical personnel during the Famine also needed to be very brave as the mortality rate from cholera in Westport was 44.4% and in Ballinrobe 51.8%. Within the Workhouses, some inmates also undertook menial nursing duties and were often in charge of patients' clothing, cleaning and mending. Posts in nursing came to be highly valued after the Famine and became very popular as a career choice among girls.

A few ladies achieved the position of Matron, 3 of Public Institutions and 3 as Matrons of Gaols in 1851. As well as administrative duties, the post of matron involved elementary instruction of female prisoners in reading and writing. To achieve such a position, one needed a relatively wealthy family or perhaps wealthy friends to undertake the financial conditions attached to the post. The advertisement for the post of Matron for Ballinrobe Union in *The Mayo Constitution* of July 10, 1849 reads as follows: 'Active intelligent person of business like habits. Also two solvent securities who will join her in a bond in the sum of £100 for the due and faithful performance of her duties'. The post of matron was interesting for several reasons; there was a high turnover in personnel despite the high salary attached to the post and because some of these ladies were married.

In 1850, Mary Bell was Mistress of Westport Workhouse,[42] Anne Miller was employed in a similar capacity in Ballina. At this time, George Rogers and Mrs. Rogers were Master and Mistress of the Workhouse at Belmullet. Mrs. Rogers was still there in 1853, but a new Master had been appointed. In 1853, Mary Bell was succeeded as Mistress of the Westport Workhouse by Rose Kilgariff. In 1853, the Master and Mistress of Swinford Workhouse were John and Mrs. Carroll. Some people remained in the same post, such as Eliza Plunkett who was Mistress in Castlebar in 1850 and was still there in 1853. One wonders if brothers and sisters were sometimes appointed as Master and

---

[41]   Devon Commission, Part II, 1848, pp. 1000–1001.
[42]   *Thom's Directories 1850–1853.*

Mistress, such as the appointment at Killala of John J. Jones and Christiana Jones.

Working relations between Masters and Mistresses were fraught on occasions and could work to the detriment of their charges, as in the Gaol of Castlebar where the misunderstandings between the Governor and Mrs. Kendellen, the Matron,[43] became matter for official comment and report.

Women sometimes obtained minor Civil Service posts. Of 8 Stamp Distributors in Mayo in 1850, 2 were women, Mrs. Duff of Ballaghaderreen and Mrs. Kelly of Westport. By the year 1851, 9 Postmistresses had been appointed.

In the field of teaching much progress had been made. Though no female inspectors had been appointed by 1851, positions in education provided many jobs. In 1826, there were 41 female teachers in the County, 23 of them Catholics.[44] By 1841, there were 150 female and 285 male teachers in the County as well as 14 governesses.[45] In the year 1842, we learn that there were 63 male and 11 female teachers employed in National Schools, so teachers were employed in a great variety of teaching establishments in the County. By 1851, 167 ladies were employed as teachers. Although male teachers outnumbered female teachers by almost 2 to 1 in that year, much solid progress had been made in this field. Posts in both nursing and education were regarded as 'respectable', conferring security and status in the locality on girls who held these positions.

In Church affairs, women of all religious denominations played a minor part in official positions, with no female Ministers of Religion but 3 posts as sextons. One must remember the hidden life lived by women motivated by the highest religious principles who provided much Famine relief and helped to improve the quality of life of the poor. By 1851, there were 20 Sisters of Mercy and Charity in Mayo, who by visiting the sick,

---

43 *Mayo Constitution*, 25th November, 1844.
44 Appendix to Second Report from the Commissioners of Irish Education Inquiry. Appendix No. 22. pp. 1256–1280.
45 Famine Relief papers, Vol. VI. Table F, p. 216.

providing education and fostering the campaign of Fr. Matthew to promote Temperance greatly improved the lives of the poor.

Many women were employed, at least for short term periods, on Famine Relief schemes set up by individuals, or by organizations supported by the Society of Friends. Some also broke stones on the roads for 4*d*. a day on the Public Works. 430 women were employed in such work on Nov. 7th 1846, and in Feb. 1847, 2,783 women were employed in this capacity.[46] Women were not employed on the drainage schemes set up by the Public Works although some were employed on drainage works begun by individuals such as Col. Vaughan Jackson who had received grants for land reclamation works.

In general, women workers received lower wages than men doing similar work. In 1836, the standard rate ranged from 2d. to 4*d*. a day, for women working in the fields on seasonal labor. Industrial wages were not much higher. Hay Bros. paid 4*d*. a day to girls and boys working in their flax rettery and from 7*d*. to 2*s*. to men.[47] Women in the cotton factory in Westport received from 2*d*. to 4*d*. a day,[48] a self-employed dressmaker could earn 1/- a day,[49] while many living by spinning had to be content to work for 2*d*. and their food.[50]

We have a reasonably good knowledge of the salaries paid to teachers, although a great variety of conditions was the norm for education in Mayo in 1826. This refers both to the type and foundation of schools and working conditions and salaries for teachers. Alicia Keogh, who taught in a poor cabin, earned £12 per annum.[51] Maria McKeon, who was employed by the London Hibernian Society, was paid according to the proficiency of the pupils. At Doonfeeney in 1835, Brigid Ormsby received a salary of £12 per annum from the Baptist Society. There does not

---

[46] Famine Relief Papers: Board of Works Series, 2nd Part, London, 1847, p. 49.

[47] *Transactions*, Appendix XX, p. 435.

[48] Appendix D, p. 24.

[49] Appendix A, p. 378.

[50] Ibid., p. 124.

[51] Appendix 22, 1826 Education Report, p. 1256.

seem to have been any real increase in teachers' salaries between 1826 and 1835, at least for those teachers receiving stipends from religious societies. In this year, Ann McDonough had 54 pupils on roll, who paid from 1s. to 1s. 3d. each. If she had no bad debts, her salary amounted to approximately £2. 14s. 0d. per quarter.[52] In 1838, the pupils of Kilgellu paid their teacher from 1s. to 2s. 6d. per quarter. If all her 70 pupils paid their fees, this lady received between £3. 10s. 0d. and £8. 15s. 0d. per quarter.[53] In 1842, under the National School System, the salaries for male teachers ranged from £12 to £20; those for female teachers from £10 to £15 according to grade. Mistresses who taught needlework received a salary of £6 p.a.[54] A local subscription was often collected to supplement the teacher's salary, but at least they could count on the regularity of payment of the 'Queen's wages'.

Matrons of Public Institutions were paid adequate salaries, according to the standard of the times. The post of matron of the Ballinrobe Workhouse carried a salary of £35 p.a. in the year 1849.[55] The fringe benefits attached to this position were 'apartments and lodgings'. Yet the post of Master carried a much higher wage. In 1849, the Master of Castlebar Union Workhouse received a salary of £60 p.a. of the 'Queen's wages'.

By 1851, women were beginning to gain positions in business, albeit in humble positions. For example, the agent for Castlebar for John Cassell's Coffee was Mrs. Young, a stationer in Market Street.[56]

The lives of women in this period were bedevilled by the twin scourges of Famine and unemployment. When one takes into account the number of women in Public Institutions, including one third of the widows of the County as well as the number of female beggars in 1851, 2,408 women as against 722 men, one begins to realize the magnitude of the problem. In the Barony

---

[52] Commission of Public Instruction, 1835, p. 86d.
[53] O.S. Field Books, Mayo. Dublin 1838, p. 340.
[54] 9th Report: Commissioners of National Education in Ireland, 1834–1842 inclusive, Dublin 1844.
[55] *Mayo Constitution*, July 7th, 1849.
[56] Ibid., July 17th, 1849.

of Tirawley in 1851, in every parish, the number of women not having specified occupation vastly outnumbered the many men who were employed. Female unemployment was particularly bad in Ardagh and Kilfian, where unemployed women outnumbered unemployed men by 14 to 1, in Kilbelfad by almost 13 to 1 and in Ballinahaglish by 12 to 1. Many women were reduced to begging. In the tragic circumstances of the time, several failed to support themselves by begging and much of the tragedy of poverty and unemployment is revealed in the story of the Workhouses.

While making allowances for the infirm and aged in these institutions, the proportion of able-bodied out of work women in them was very high. Many of these women were accommodated in the Auxiliary Workhouses. The lowest figure for women in Auxiliary Workhouses was 43% recorded in the Ballina Union in 1851. In the Auxiliary Workhouse in Castlebar, there were 50 men and 515 women. In Belmullet, 76% of the inmates of the Main Workhouse and 90% of the population of the first Auxiliary Workhouse were women. There were no women, however, in the second Auxiliary Workhouse. The occupants of the main Workhouse in Westport were 66% women and they also comprised 98% of the inmates of the Auxiliary Workhouse where there were only 3 men. To show how bleak economic conditions were in Westport, we must remember that women formed the largest proportion, not only of the main and first Auxiliary Workhouses but also over half of the second Auxiliary Workhouse.

The problem of female unemployment was an ongoing one, and there were still large numbers of women in Public Institutions in 1860, when attempts were organized to transport some of these women to Australia to work as servants thus reducing the burden on the Poor Rate at home, Even in 1862, there were 138 paupers in the Workhouse in Belmullet, an increase of 42 over the previous year. Of these 32 were able-bodied paupers, 9 males and 23 fernales.[57] Some emigrated to

---

57 Saunder's Newsletter, 29th September, 1862.

England, Scotland and the United States in an attempt to find employment.

In spite of both unemployment and the changing employment patterns, women had adapted well to the changing economic circumstances of the period. Thus, when the textile industry in its various branches went into decline, there was a sizeable increase in the numbers of women who became involved in egg and fowl dealing, selling fish and all manner of trading to support themselves. Lack of education and training may have hindered some women from obtaining employment. It was certainly felt that it was a major cause of crime among women. Some women who had skills were hindered by lack of cash from providing for themselves. A laborer in Burrishoole stated: 'My wife used to help me by weaving; she has no work now and has not the means of purchasing yarn to make work for herself.'[58] Organizations, such as the Society of Friends, while ministering to starving people by providing them with food, realized that what women in Mayo, as elsewhere, needed was not a hand-out, but 'permanent relief' – jobs by which they could support themselves.

Women's wages were very important to the economy of the family. They helped to pay the rent. Walter Jenny of Cong, whose late wife had been a dressmaker, stated that when his wife lived, he had been decent and fit to appear before a congregation.[59] Women, who endured the hardship of breaking stones on the Public Relief Works, often kept entire families alive by their efforts. Some, reduced to begging, also did likewise. We learn that in Derrygarriff, Hugh Moran with a sickly wife unable to go out herself to beg and their four children were supported by the beggary of his mother-in-law.[60] If the wife of a migratory laborer did not 'take to the bag', she was probably very busy tending whatever crops her husband planted before leaving the country or attempting to save turf for

---

[58] Appendix A, p. 374. Evidence of Thomas Gallaher.
[59] Ibid., p. 378.
[60] Ibid., p. 499.

the Winter fuel supplies. Other women, particularly widows, attempted to procure a living for themselves from the produce of their gardens. It is certain that women's labor contributed to the family wealth, whether by direct labor, begging or helping on the farm. Where women had regular employment, they used their wages to good effect. Their appearance improved, they bought furniture and above all, they effected a change in diet, with much less dependence on the potato.[61]

By 1851, many women who had survived the tragedy of the Famine must have been very depressed by the continuing lack of employment, with the consequent poverty, and loss of self-respect which it caused in women accustomed to independent income. They had heard the death-knell of the textile industry, with no apparent possibility of recovery. For those who could not obtain jobs in service, emigration beckoned, with drastic effects on the dynamics of the life of the parish which they left. If one examines the Parish Register of Foxford from 1865 to 1890, one can trace much emigration in the Parish. Few girls born in this parish from 1845 to 1850 married in the parish or even in Ireland. They married in the large cities of England, such as London, Liverpool, Birmingham and in the main east coast cities of the U.S.A., at much older ages than was the pattern before the Famine.

For those who remained at home and who had sufficient family resources, the emphasis was on obtaining a permanent pensionable job, thus assuring a regular income for one's lifetime. Women's wages supported households and often provided the means of obtaining education for other members of the family. Education became important for women and was seen as a great means of social mobility. It also made girls more eligible. Unemployment not only contributed to poverty, it also was a major factor in delaying marriage if a girl had no dowry. Paradoxically, the whole matter of women's employment had become more important at a time when job opportunities had

---

[61] *Transactions*: Appendix XIX and Report from Arthur Barrington.

become fewer. This trend continued into the twentieth century so that by 1911, one working woman in three was a servant, while another large group was employed in agriculture.[62] This continued under native Governments, so that in 1926, six out of ten of the 329,000 women at work were either in farming or domestic service, while fewer than one in ten worked in industry.[63]

Thus, it can be seen that the whole question of female employment was of great moment to women, chiefly because of the lack of job opportunities from 1800 on. While difficulties in getting and keeping employment were exacerbated by the Famine, the Industrial Revolution and the decrease in effective demand for the goods produced by women, one should not forget that the whole question of providing jobs for women or indeed of women being self-employed has been fraught with difficulty and that women with the limited wages which they were able to earn, made an outstanding economic contribution to the welfare of their families and of their community.

---

[62] Census Ireland 1911, General Report Table 19.
[63] Irish Congress of Trade Unions, (ICTU) Trade Union Information, September, 1968, pp. 2–3.

20. National Famine Memorial at Murrisk. This statue, in the form of
a coffin ship, sculpted by John Behan was unveiled by President Mary
Robinson on 20 July 1997.

The inscription reads as follows:

To honour the memory of all, who died suffered
and emigrated due to the Great Famine of 1845–1850
and the victims of all famines.

6

Migration

In the earlier years of this study, there was much migration, particularly among men. In 1841, migrants from Mayo comprised almost 40% of the Connacht migrants.[1] Of particular interest is how women and children came to terms with this fact.

Migration was a live issue in the first half of the nineteenth century. Up to 1810, there was a growing demand in Great Britain for outside agricultural labor which coincided with reduced employment in Ireland. This extra demand was a boon to harassed men, their wives and families. A new system of agriculture was evolving in England which involved two principal figures, the large farmer and the hired day labourer.[2] Irish immigrants were welcomed by landowners because, besides supplying the farmer with more efficient labor (than the local village paupers), they also relieved them of the onus of supporting the parish laborers who, when the temporary employment was over, would become burdens on the Poor Rate. This attitude of welcome did not extend to the native laborers on the mainland who felt threatened by Irish migrants, both men and women, who were landed by steam boats in places such as the very heart of Scotland near the agricultural districts.[3]

This prejudice against western migrants also occurred in Ireland among the workers of the South East who regarded them as 'dirty pool-dwellers, bog trotters, mountaineers without self-respect or manners'.[4] Many a sensitive woman, who had gone to

---

[1] British Parliamentary Papers, Vol. 2.
[2] Kerr, Barbara: Irish Seasonal Migration to Great Britain 1800–1838, Irish Historical Studies Vol. III, 1942–1943.
[3] Report on Irish Poor, 1836. Evidence of Mr. McNeel, p. 151.
[4] Súilleabháin, Ó. A., *Cinn-Lae Amhlaoibh Uí Shúilleabháin*, pp. 21–22.

Leinster to look for harvest work, must have cringed in the face of such derision.

Women in Mayo were particularly affected by migration, as migrants left the County at the rate of 1 in 37 of its inhabitants in 1851.[5] Whether wives remained at home with their children or accompanied their husbands, they endured great hardships. There were great variations within the County, however. Very few migrated from Lacken or Killala.[6] In districts such as Crossmolina[7] and Cong[8], most migrants were unmarried men. Witnesses for Doonfeeney gave us a confused picture of the incidence of migration, ranging from very few to very many.[9] In Kilfian, 61 men migrated, 57 of whom were married.[10] When one considers the large number of widows in this parish, one cannot but sympathize with the women who carried a very heavy burden of agricultural work as well as ordinary domestic duties. Along the sea-board, as at Aughavale, mainly married men migrated,[11] and half of the married men of Castlemore.[12] In relatively prosperous areas of the County, such as Ballyheane, Aglish, Ballintubber and Borriscarra, approximately one third of the married men migrated.

'It was the custom for the harvester's wife and family to remain in Ireland and beg in the more opulent counties'.[13] This practice was not universal. Many women stayed in or very close to their homes, particularly if their husbands provided for them, even partially, in their absence. Many migratory men made gallant efforts to provide provisions for their wives and families, a difficult task in a cash starved economy. A migrant from Mayo needed at least £1 for the journey to England, before making any

---

5   Census Ireland 1841, Vol. 2, p xxvii.
6   Supplement to Appendix A, p. 32.
7   Ibid. Evidence of A. Ormsby, p. 30.
8   Ibid. Evidence of John Fynn, J.P., p. 27.
9   Ibid. Evidence of Rev. Fr. Hart, Rev. Francis Little, John Faussett, p. 30.
10 Ibid. Evidence of Rev. M. Conway, p. 31.
11 Ibid. Evidence of Wm. Patten, p. 29.
12 Ibid. Evidence of Rev. B. Durcan, p. 24.
13 First Report from His Majesty's Commissioners for the Inquiry into the condition of the poorer classes in Ireland, 1835. H.C. 369, p. 379.

provision for those at home.[14] In some instances, husbands did not make provision for wives and families before migrating, not through malice but because they feared failing to meet future financial commitments, as the husband's earnings were required to pay the rent. We hear of the plight of men who could not depend on relatives or neighbors to help in their absence. In this situation, they took as much provision as would support their families during their absence from some independent neighbor, giving him some 30–35% interest and security to pay to the last farthing as soon as they returned.[15] Others managed to leave provisions for a portion of their absence, the usual practice in Kilcoleman.[16] When these provisions ran out, women and children resorted to begging. These could count themselves fortunate, when contrasted with the women for whom no provision was made.

In large areas of the County, such as Doonfeeney,[17] Kilmaine[18] and Aughagower,[19] women resorted to begging. In parts of Aughavale, in the absence of the men, women and children shut up their houses and took to the roads.[20] Some resorted to begging only when their potato supplies ran out.[21] A number who stayed in their cabins lived on one scant meal a day rather than beg.[22] Others depended on the help of friends and relatives.

Some women tried to be self-sufficient and provide food for themselves. Some women, particularly in Borriscarra and Ballintubber, lived on the produce of their gardens which contained from a rood to an acre in general.[23] Others lived on the produce of their little farms or conacre.[24] Some wives in

---

14 Ibid., pp. 572–573.
15 Supplement to Appendix A. Evidence of Rev. David Jennings, p. 23.
16 Ibid. Evidence of Henry Brown, p. 24.
17 Ibid., p. 30.
18 Ibid. Evidence of Rev. E. Whelan, p. 27.
19 Ibid. Evidence of Rev. Peter Ward, p. 21.
20 Ibid. Evidence of Wm. Patten, p. 29.
21 Ibid. Evidence of Rev. P. Gibbons and Rev. R. Creighton, p. 22.
22 Ibid., p. 24 (Kilmovee).
23 Ibid. Evidence of Rev. John Kirby, p. 23.
24 Ibid., p. 29.

Kilmaclash were left with a sufficient quantity of potatoes to sustain them in their husbands' absence.[25] Of interest is the report for Castlebar or Aglish where the wives and children lived on the provisions in store for the year. Formerly, these women used to beg.[26] The position at Balla, just a few miles away, provided a stark contrast. In this place, migrant laborers 'left their wives in misery at home'.[27] Some families in desperation resorted to the Workhouses as a temporary measure and even pawned their clothes before entering them.

In Westport Workhouse in June 1850, Forbes learned that 'no fewer than 300 children had gone out of the house in consequence of money received from their fathers in England and Scotland and 21 had gone to America through funds sent home to them by their relations. In fact, when wives left the Workhouses to join their husbands on their return, many older girls were unwilling to leave them'.[28] See Chapter on the Famine.

Some women migrated, not only to other parts of Ireland but to other countries, particularly during the Famine. Referring particularly to the Unions of Ballinrobe, Castlebar and Westport, it was stated: 'Experience proves that large numbers of both men and women migrate to other lands to seek employment and endure much hardship and privation in order to accumulate a small hoard with which they return to their families'.[29] Widows worked as migratory laborers in Scotland and on occasions, received free passage on the boats, as may be inferred from the evidence of Pat Cooper. 'My wife and children came with me (to Scotland) but they did not pretend to belong to me. They pretended to be a widow and orphans and got their passage in charity. In Scotland we separated every day, I to look

---

[25] Ibid., p. 21.

[26] Supplement to Appendix A, p. 22. Evidence of Lieut. Col. James M'Alpine.

[27] Ibid. Evidence of Rev. P. Nolan, p. 23.

[28] Forbes, J., *Memorandums*, pp. 275 et seq.

[29] Messrs. Lecky and Thomas Casey, Vice Guardians to the Poor Law Commissioners, August 21, 1847. I.U.P. Series of British Parliamentary Papers, 4th Series – Famine (Ireland). Vol. 2 – 1847–1848.

for work and they to beg and we met every evening. We were better off begging in Ireland than in Scotland, but we got better food and more of it in Scotland, but we could get no lodging'.[30]

While many migratory laborers returned to Ireland, some attempted to remain in Scotland and received no great welcome from the authorities. Bishop Gillis of Edinburgh spoke of the refusal by the authorities to grant outdoor relief to poor parents – 'widows with children of wives whose husbands had gone in search of work – while insisting on their children being taken into the Workhouse where they were not allowed to attend Mass and where they became victims of proselytism'.[31] Some managed to get a foothold in Scotland and we read of immigrant Irish women and children in the mines.[32] In Achill, there was a tradition of women migrating to Scotland and working in the fields along with their husbands. There would also seem to have been a pattern of either transhumance or of whole villages going begging on this island. Achill Island had several clusters of houses, varying from 20 to 80. Some were summer residences only and were entirely deserted in the Winter – others were Winter residences only and deserted in Summer.[33] This pattern of migration, already well established in 1832, was common in Scotland in 1893[34] and it continued on into the twentieth century.

Women lived harsh, difficult lives in the absence of their menfolk, especially if they had to beg during the Summer or Famine months. The burden of supporting these women and children fell almost entirely on the small farmer, who found himself in very difficult circumstances.[35] For those able to remain in their cabins, life was grim with several subsisting on one scant

---

30 Appendix A, p. 368.
31 Evidence of Bishop Gillis, Catholic Coadjutor Bishop of Edinburgh – March 1843, cited in *The Irish in Scotland 1798–1845*.
32 Handley, James, op. cit. p. 210.
33 Magazine of Natural History. Account of Edward Newman quoted in *The Way that I went* by Lloyd Praeger, p. 192.
34 Royal Commission on Labour: Agricultural Labourers (Ireland) 1893–4, Vol. 37, Part 1.
35 Kerr, Barbara, op. cit. p. 380.

meal a day, and many doing the heavy Summer work with crops and turf in rural areas. Matters were made more difficult for some of them as in some cases, grown boys, who might have helped their mothers, also accompanied their fathers when they migrated, a very strong custom in Kilcoleman.[36] Yet the lives of the women who could remain in their cabins were much less difficult than the lives of those forced to shut up their cabins and beg. In such cases, holdings were neglected and the family generally faced a cold miserable winter as no fuel was saved. The difficult situation was exacerbated, if absent husbands could not earn as much as might pay the rent and extra expenses caused by the dearth of potatoes and turf. An extreme case of this was seen in Kilfian parish in 1835. Some migrant men were forced to pawn their clothes to return there in a very short time.[37] The hardship was aggravated because most people lacked a change of clothing and almost inevitable eviction faced these people that Winter as the hardship began to bite. Indeed, 400 families left the parish over a short period of time.

One can only guess at the strain imposed on many marriages by migration. Migration sometimes led to desertion, particularly during the Famine. In some cases, many deserted wives had to resort to the Workhouses. Yet many men faithfully remitted money to Ireland, so that their wives and children could leave these Workhouses. One also wonders about the break-up of village life during the busiest seasons of the year.

Many questions remain unanswered about the care of people and belongings left behind, when whole families left their holdings. It is unlikely that old people wandered very far from home to beg. Who cared for these people when younger family members begged in distant parts of the country? One also wonders about the care of animals and fowl. Grown fowl may perhaps have been left to forage for themselves. One can imagine a kindly neighbor caring for young chickens, goslings, etc., in the absence of the family. When one considers how

---

[36] Supplement to Appendix A. Evidence of Rev. M. Conway, p. 31.
[37] Appendix A. Evidence of Rev. W. Hughes, p. 375.

important fowl and eggs were in providing income for women, it is unlikely they were left to fend for themselves. It would appear that some kind relative or neighbor milked cows and may have acted in a caretaker capacity to maintain whatever animals the family might have. The case of animals, however, may have posed fewer problems than might be supposed. In Burrishoole, it was reckoned that almost half of the population of 917 families had no cow.[38]

There was little public outcry in Ireland against seasonal migration which inflicted hardship on so many people, even though it bolstered a system tottering on the brink of disaster. After 1815 in particular, when the slump in agricultural prices should have led to a reduction in the rents for agricultural land, the reality was that the Irish landlords were able to keep the rents unnaturally high, beyond the real value of the land, by the profits of annual migration.[39] It was against the interest of the landlords, many of them absentees, to attempt to reform the evil land system, of which they were the chief beneficiaries and it was this evil land system that led to seasonal migration.

One can but pity the victims of such a system. The novelist Maria Edgeworth empathized with their lot, describing as 'poor crayturs' (creatures) the poor womenfolk of migrant Connacht farm workers.[40] One can but admire the buoyancy of spirit which enabled women to cope, when the extra burdens caused by migration aggravated the very difficult circumstances of their lives.

---

[38] Third Report Emigration 1827.
[39] Ibid.
[40] Edgeworth, Maria, *The Absentee*, p. 46.

John Meenaghan and Ellen O'Toole   8 November 1903

21. Wedding in Ballintubber, 1903.

7

Marriage

Many marriages contracted in Mayo during this period were youthful and improvident, particularly among the poor. It was stated that the greater proportion of the poorer class will be found married before 20 and many women do not wait beyond 15.[1] It was stated of such marriages that perhaps they had not two pence provided to meet the wants that attended on marriage.[2]

One is amazed to learn that marriages took place at earlier ages among the very poor. This was explained as follows: 'If a man is very poor, he expects nothing but poverty with a wife and his choice is soon made, but if he had any kind of opulence, or if he expects to have it he takes his time and looks about for a wife that will add to it'.[3] By contrast, the very poor married if they had enough potatoes for a year.[4] This reckless indifference to the means of providing for a family was particularly noted among the laborers,[5] of whom it was said that the poorer the man, the earlier he married. It was felt that illicit distillation helped to foster improvident marriages by making people less wise, less prudent, less cautious in contracting such marriages.[6]

In 1834, we get a picture of a rather shiftless people in Mayo who were irresponsible in their attitudes to marriage, particularly in Erris. 'When they marry – for Malthus and restrictions upon

[1] House of Commons: Parliamentary Papers, Vol. XXXI, 1836. Appendix D, p. 12. Evidence of Sr. S. O'Malley, Bart.
[2] Ibid. Evidence of William Ormsby, p. 28.
[3] House of Commons: Parliamentary Papers, p. 364. Appendix A. Evidence of Mr. M'Nally and Michael Hynes, p. 379.
[4] Appendix A. Evidence of Rev. Mr. Lyons, later Dean Lyons, p. 386.
[5] Appendix A., p. 370.
[6] Johnson, James, *A Tour in Ireland*, 1844, p. 169.

population are no more recognized in Erris than the Pope is
by a modern Methodist – they will obtain a patch of mountain
from the patron, erect a cabin, construct a still and, setting all
political dogmas at defiance, then and there brew the most
excellent whiskey and add to the seven millions (population)
considerably'.[7] There is no doubt that persons engaged in the
trade were enabled to pay high rents and this fostered early
marriages.[8]

Parents did little to hinder early marriages. There were men
anxious to marry off grown up daughters to have 'someone
else to do for them'.[9] Some parents actually resorted to deceit
in order to get their daughters married. Some, unscrupulous
or harassed, promised a dowry, which they has no intention of
paying, on the occasion of a daughter's marriage. 'He (the father)
will promise £1 with her when he cannot give her a penny and,
once she is off his hands, let her husband shift to support her'.
Many young men were not really gulled by such promises but
felt they had nothing to lose by marriage as 'if he (the husband)
has no work, if he is ashamed to beg for himself; the wife and
children will beg and support him'.[10] A laborer in Kilmore Erris
tells us: 'I married a wife and was promised the foal in the mare's
belly as a fortune. The mare quickly foaled and from that day to
this, I never got as much as a noggin to hold a drop of water in
by my wife'.[11]

A measure of the prevailing grinding poverty is the fact that
the chance of a foal or a calf is thought a fine thing as a dowry.
Many married on the promise of a lamb before the ewe was
tupped at all.[12] This poverty continued to haunt some couples
and marriage often led people into beggary. One account
affirmed: 'I never knew a beggar marry with the intention of
continuing to beg though they are often reduced to beggary soon

7   Maxwell, W.H., *Wild Sports in the West*, 1834, p. 100. Dublin n.d.
8   Poor Inquiry Ireland. Appendix E. 1836, Vol. XXXIII, p. 23.
9   Appendix A., p. 370.
10   Ibid., p. 370.
11   Ibid., p. 386. Evidence of Dominic Frehill.
12   Ibid., p. 386. Evidence of Edward Burke.

22. Seaside section of Dooagh Village.

after marriage,[13] which they hoped might be a temporary phase of their lives'. Beggars never married intending to continue to beg with the exception of tinkers' families.[14]

Mercenary considerations seem to have been a potent motive for marriage, particularly among the poor, who were anxious to improve their condition. 'A young man will marry a servant for

[13]   Ibid., p. 364. Evidence of Edward M'Nally.
[14]   Ibid., p. 505.

the few shillings of wages she may have saved, as a drowning man will catch at a straw'.[15] Other factors exerted a powerful influence. Both men and women, more advanced in years, often assigned it as their motive for marrying in their impoverished circumstances that they might have children to care for them in old age.

One can gauge how strong the wish to marry was among some girls, when one studies cases tried for rape. These cases were often used by girls to compel unwilling gentlemen into marriage, particularly as convictions for rape carried the death penalty and when, or if commuted, carried a sentence of a long term of transportation. Frequently, rape charges were dropped on the marriage of the parties.[16] Such cases had become more frequent around 1835, since some men had lately been executed for rape. In 5 months, five or six such cases had occurred in the Cong district.[17] In Kilmore Erris, the Parish Priest was confident that 9 out of 10 cases were fictitious – got up merely for the purpose of forcing marriage[18] – the so-called 'out-of-dock marriage'. Courts were distinctly suspicious in cases of alleged rape and in the Castlebar Assizes in 1835, one notices that although 25 rape cases were heard, only 3 men were convicted of this charge and were duly sent to death.[19]

Unmarried mothers generally found their matrimonial prospects blighted, unless the girl had a much larger dowry than usual.[20] Generally, not more than 1 in 10 got married.[21]

The only staying factor in delaying marriages among the poorest seems to have been the difficulty in making up marriage fees.[22] This was not an insuperable factor, however, and some parish registers carry rare entries designated N.P. (not paid)

[15] Ibid., p. 374. Evidence of Mr. Butler.
[16] Ibid., p. 52. Evidence of Mr. Crampton.
[17] Ibid., p. 52.
[18] Ibid., p. 53, Evidence of Fr. Lyons, afterwards Dean Lyons.
[19] British Parliamentary Papers, 1835. Vol. XLV. Committals Ireland.
[20] Appendix A, p. 53.
[21] Ibid., p. 53.
[22] Ibid., p. 374. Evidence of Rev. W. Hughes, P.P.

or else paid in instalments.[23] The Crossmolina parish register reveals several marriages for which fees were not received in 1833, and even mentions one couple who had flitted one year after matrimony, without paying any fees. Registers for Kilfian and Crossmolina reveal very few marriages during 1846 and 1847, all marked paid. Clearly, only the better off married during these years.

The Census figures for 1841 and 1851 reveal many interesting changes which occurred in the decade:

Number of women who were unmarried, married and widowed for the whole of the county in 1841 and 1851

Unmarried		Married		Widowed	
1841	**1851**	**1841**	**1851**	**1841**	**1851**
34,082	29,920	59,756	36,502	12,902	14,435

Source: 1851 Census – Pages 576–578

The number of unmarried women in Mayo was lower than that in Connacht and in Ireland as a whole. The number of unmarried women decreased considerably between 1841 and 1851. This may reflect the number of young women who died, emigrated or who delayed marriage. There was a greater decline in the number of married women though. Parish Registers reveal that only the comparatively wealthy were getting married since the onset of the famine. The number of widows increased dramatically in this decade, when the ratio of widows to widowers was about 3 to 1. By 1851, the pattern of later marriages among women had begun, when three times as many men as women between the ages of 17 and 24 married. Some of these young men may have married older women. By 1851, most women who married were between the ages of 35 and 54, with few over 54 getting married or remarried in either town or country.[24]

---

[23] Crossmolina Parish Register. (I am indebted to the late, great Tony Donohoe for his insights into this Register).

[24] British Parl. Papers. Vol. XIV 1951, General Report (xlii).

In 1851, there were no widows under 17. However, the rate of widowhood was very high for both men (6,900) and women (495) over 54, a striking contrast with the figures for the County as a whole.[25] Widowers who remarried were usually below the age of 54, though one man aged seventy married in 1846 in Crossmolina, 'having been a widower for many years'.[26]

Love, as in all ages, was a potent motive for marriage but several other considerations prompted marriage. Marriage conferred status as 'neither man nor woman reached full status in the rural community until they were married'.[27] A married woman of twenty had a more important position in life than that of a spinster of fifty and marriage meant a settled life and a degree of independence unknown outside of it.[28] A spinster of forty five was practically nobody[29] in the community, and the resentment of the unmarried bachelors and spinsters was shown in such customs as 'throwing salt on them at Shrove to preserve them until the following Shrove',[30] which was a popular time for marriage. Traditionally, in Ireland, a wife had complete control of the dwelling house and the fowl. A married woman, however young, had authority in the home over her unmarried sister, unmarried sister-in-law, children. This authority conferred a status on married women which was precious to them.

The lot of the unmarried girl was made more difficult at this time as employment for women had declined, particularly in the cottage industries. Such girls became more dependent on their parents or, perhaps, were given a grudging toleration in a brother's or sister's household. The deterioration in women's economic women also affected their marriage prospects. Marriage was viable for a poor man when his wife could earn money by knitting or spinning or by agricultural labor to eke

---

[25] Ibid.
[26] Crossmolina Parish Register.
[27] Danaher, Kevin, *In Ireland Long Ago*, p. 158.
[28] Ibid., p. 159.
[29] Danaher, Kevin, Some Marriage Customs and their Regional Distribution'. *Béaloideas*, IM 42–44, p. 170.
[30] Ibid., p. 175.

23. Another view of Dooagh Village, showing beautiful beach and mountain scenery, with low houses built at right angles to the sea, the cocks of hay tied down with '*súgáns*' (straw ropes), stone walls and some ruins.

out his earnings. As the nineteenth century progressed, this was less the case, with less of a chance of young people establishing independent households without parental support. Thus the dowry became more important as the period progressed. 'As the wife made a lesser economic contribution in current terms to the household, the amount of capital she brought with her assumed greater importance. Because the daughter had little to bring except the dowry she got from her father, her marriage prospects now depended completely on him and, in many cases, she had to abide by his wishes.[31] The lack of a dowry caused many girls to remain unmarried.

As well as a natural love of children, Irish women looked to children to provide them with security for their old age. The birth rate was high but so was the infant mortality rate and many women lost children, particularly in the first year of life. There were some interesting variations in the number of births between the years 1832 and 1841, with an overall decrease noted, with a huge decrease in Connacht, which may be accounted for by the large drop in the number of girls who married under the age of 17 in that period.[32]

One wonders how happy some of the marriages were, or what the expectations of marriage were in some cases. While not expressly stated, there seems to have been an idea that any marriage was better than none, even an 'out-of-dock' marriage, a reprehensible practice which continued long after the period in question. A wry entry beside a payment for marriage fees in the Crossmolina Parish Register reads 'rape up to this'. Perhaps, in some cases, men harbored resentment which may have led to desertion and to many cases of assault, particularly if they were compelled to marry a woman, whom they would not wish to marry under normal circumstances.

In many marriages, there were elements now recognized by sociologists as major factors in contributing to marriage breakdown – lack of privacy, poverty, economic insecurity, cramped living quarters, and poor facilities within the home, among others. Extra strain was placed on many marriages by migration. There must have been much strain on many women

---

[31] Lee, J.J., 'Women and the Church since the Famine', p. 37. *Women in Irish Society: The Historical Dimension* eds. Margaret McCurtain and Donncha Ó Corráin.

[32] 1841 Census, Births.

trying to cope with the demands of both young and old people within the home. Matters were aggravated, if a marriage partner was addicted to alcohol, had violent tendencies or suffered from physical or mental illness. This strain was compounded, if there was a cantankerous old person in the household as well. The Famine dealt a death blow to many marriages. While there had always been a trickle of marriages wrecked by desertion, there was a sizeable increase in the number of deserted wives in Workhouses, such as Swinford.[33] These husbands had migrated to England or America and had not returned. It was also stated that 'the bonds of mutual affection are loosening under the pressure of want and husbands have deserted their wives and children.'[34] Not all deserting husbands left the jurisdiction, however, and some set up other households here. In general, such a man felt he could do so with impunity, as it was most unlikely that a wife would take him to Court for maintenance, as she would have none to get, because of the erring husband's poverty. However, two men were charged with bigamy at the Castlebar Assizes, which tells us that not all erring husbands got away scotfree. Many deserted wives had to go to the Workhouse, and if a deserting husband had means, the Workhouse authorities might bring him to Court to attempt to enforce maintenance. One celebrated case of this type was reported in The Mayo Constitution of December 23rd, 1841. It referred to George Carr, a soldier whose service was about to be applied for to support a woman who was admitted to Castlebar Workhouse, a short time previously. He presented himself to explain to the satisfaction of the Court that she was not his wife. In an elaborate statement of his case, he admitted that he was told he got married in a state of drunkenness. He admitted that this woman had lived with him for several years, by whom he had a son, but that from her conduct while abroad, he was obliged to send her home as a disgraced woman. The Court decided that

---

33 6th Series I.U.P. British Parl. Papers: Famine Ireland, 1847–1848, p. 410. Letter of Mr. Gibbons.
34 Pim, Jonathan, *Transactions*, p. 263.

he was married, and his wife got support for 5/-. He obviously resented paying this as he brought the matter to Court again the following year in an attempt to have the Court Order quashed.

It would seem reasonable to expect that there was particular strain on the marriages where either partner became prisoner, particularly if the prison sentence was for a crime regarded as unsocial. Laborers often did tillage on Sundays and holydays for the wives of short-term prisoners; this practice does not seem to have applied to the wives of long-term prisoners or to the wives of men who were transported. It could be said that transportation marked the death blow to many a marriage, though some of those transported sent for their wives and children to join them, when sentences were served and the necessary means were available.

The Church aspects of marriage are discussed in the Chapter of Women and Religion. Suffice it to say that a marriage blessed with children was regarded as the ideal state by women, and marriages were great social occasions. Marriages were often held in the house where the couple was going to live and, in times of great hardship, neighbors helped out to provide full and plenty for the guests. This was important for any appearance of shortage or niggardliness at a wedding was a source of shame for all concerned,[35] and might be 'thrown up against them' by some ill-intentioned person at a fair or a market years afterwards. Women helped by tactfully supplying presents of fowl and making bread and cakes to add to the joy of the occasion. Many wedding customs expressed a hope that the married couple would have plenty. In Ballycastle, for instance, when the bride came into the house, an oatmeal cake was broken on her head – that she might never know hunger.[36]

Thus, in spite of all the uncertainties of the time, women regarded marriage as their main source of happiness. One can only have sympathy for the unmarried girl who might have wished to get married. The notion that a girl could find real

---

[35] Danaher, Kevin, *In Ireland Long Ago*, p. 154.
[36] Danaher, Kevin, *Béaloideas* IM. 42–44, p. 153.

happiness outside of marriage does not seem to have been entertained and unmarried ladies of uncertain age were objects of both pity and derision. Yet, they were not as badly off as the unmarried mother, whose chances of marriage were almost certainly blighted and who was generally the object of scorn.

24. Dún Briste (Broken Fort) off Downpatrick Head, near Ballycastle an area of great beauty, also noted for successful interdenominational co-operation to provide assistance to the needy during the Great Famine.

8

Unmarried Mothers

Among destitute women, surely the most pitiful was that of the unmarried mother, who bore the opprobrium of society for the position in which she found herself. It is difficult to quantify the incidence of illegitimacy in Ireland before the Famine, as Civil Registration was not introduced before 1864. To complicate matters, illegitimacy is rarely referred to in Parish Registers. No such difficulties present themselves in obtaining evidence of the bleak lifestyles faced by unmarried mothers.

The marriage prospects of such a girl were greatly reduced and a grim life was in store for her offspring. The bastard was looked on through life with a feeling of rejection. A small farmer would be unwilling to connect himself with him and he would not give his daughter in marriage to him 'unless he were a snug man and would take her without a portion'.[1] In Kilmore Erris, such women got married but these were cases where the father gave a much larger sum of money than he would otherwise have given as a portion in order to cover the disgrace of his daughter.[2]

What legal recourse did an unmarried mother have to obtain support for her child and herself? Very little, as there was no statute which compelled a father to provide support for his illegitimate child.[3] However, there were three legal processes which sympathetic magistrates used in effect to order the father of an illegitimate child to contribute to its support:

> (1) they might award damages for seduction, questionably proven;

---

[1]   Appendix A. Kilgeever, Evidence of Pat McDonnell, p. 53.
[2]   Ibid. Evidence of Rev. Dean Lyons, p. 53.
[3]   Kerr, D., *Peel, Priests and Politics*, p. 59.

(2) they might enforce a promise to help with the child's maintenance said by the girl who have been voluntarily made by the man;

(3) they might award damages against him for impairing the girl's earning power by making her pregnant.

The second option was the most common, with the girl herself instituting proceedings and keeping the man to his alleged promise to help maintain the child. In such cases, the father always had the right of choosing between taking the child himself or paying the wages for its support, or some alternative was generally effected when the 'child was reared' at the age of two or three years.

However, the benefit of an order to receive wages for the support of her child born out of wedlock was more apparent than real in many cases. The risk or reality of an order to pay 'wages' was an important incentive to emigrate[4] in some cases, or if the father stayed on at home, the mother could not count on getting her award, as few courts assumed the powers of sending defaulters to gaol. In Cong, there were many cases of the father marrying the woman rather than pay the wages settled by the court.[5]

To obtain an order for wages, a mother was 'required to prove some agreement, either direct or implied on the part of the reputed father, but he was permitted to disprove her testimony by any evidence he could produce.[6] An agreement might consist of some matter such as a promise to provide medical help at the birth or provision of food when the girl was expecting the baby.

The unmarried mother could not count on the support of the Court, though many magistrates were, in fact, sympathetic. Sometimes, the Courts passed moral judgments which worked against these unfortunate girls. John Flynn cites a case at Cong:[7] 'A case appeared at Ross Petty Sessions near Cong where the complaint of a female against the father of a child which she had

4   Appendix A, p. 68.
5   Ibid. Evidence of Mr. Crampton, p. 52.
6   Ibid. Evidence of Mr. Glendenning, Murrisk, p. 82.
7   Supplement to Appendix A. Evidence of John Flynn, Cong.

25. Fallmore in the Mullet Peninsula, an area decimated by the Great Famine. Attempts to improve the lot of the people later were provided, inter alia, by Assisted Emigration Schemes and the Congested Districts Board.

was dismissed by the major part of the magistrates and the female left to support it, by way of discountenancing vice'. This decision met with his disapproval, and he advocated a change in the law. He wrote: 'I consider a law which would make it compulsory on the father to support the child to be a wholesome and necessary one'. The attitude of the Courts towards women who made applications for extra illegitimate children was explained as follows: 'When a woman made a second application, we have been more cautious in giving credit to her evidence and when we have believed her, we have allowed her a smaller sum'.[8] The

8   Appendix A. Evidence of Mr. Glendenning, p. 82.

uncertain attitude of the Courts may perhaps explain why so few applications for wages appeared before the courts, even though the names of the fathers were entered in Baptism Registers. In the half barony of Erris (Kilmore Erris) with a population of 23,000, there were a mere twenty cases of applications for wages for rearing illegitimate children.[9] In Cong, there were approximately twelve cases each year of women applying for wages for the support of such children.[10]

The most distressing cases were those of mothers who failed to obtain support from the child's father and her family. When a woman was unable to obtain support for her child from the father, it depended on the kindness of her parents, whether they supported her and the child. However, she was often turned out as a disgrace to the family and obliged to beg;[11] there is evidence to suggest that some of these women sank into prostitution.[12] It would seem that the traditional generosity to women with small children begging did not apply to unmarried mothers and their children and it was stated that 'nearly all prostitutes are mothers of illegitimate children.'[13] Many parents feared this possibility and several took in such girls to prevent them 'sinking deeper into vice'.[14]

Women of all ranks of society became unmarried mothers, but some girls were more at risk than others. The rate of illegitimate births was no higher among beggars than among other sections of the population, but they were often exploited when they obtained employment. 'Beggar girls when they grew up often hired with farmers; in this situation they sometimes got illegitimate children which obliged them to become beggars again. They were more exposed to temptation in this position than girls of another class, because of the lack of family support'.[15]

---

9   Ibid. Evidence of Captain Ireland, p. 53.
10   Ibid., p. 52.
11   Ibid., p.52. Evidence of Edward McNally.
12   Ibid., p. 52.
13   Ibid., p 68.
14   Ibid., Evidence of Mr. Glendenning, p. 52.
15   Ibid. Evidence of Mr. McIlrea, p. 495.

26. Ballintober (Ballintubber) Abbey restored with a view of Croagh Patrick. The traditional pilgrimage, the *Tóchair Phádraig* continues, as pilgrims follow the traditional path which links these two Patrician shrines.

Nevertheless, most Irish girls were models of chastity and, as such, were the subject of comment by foreign visitors such as Gustave de Beaumont. One wonders at this low rate. The influence of religion combined with the influence of the priests were strong factors, but by no means the only ones in bringing about such a state of affairs. Young marriages and made matches may have influenced the pattern considerably. There were enormous social and economic pressures on women to conform to the accepted norms of conduct for unmarried women, particularly as there were few opportunities available to women save in marriage. Legal considerations also reinforced the prevailing social and economic climate as there was a lack of a Bastard Law and, until 1838, a Poor Law which might lessen the hardships faced by unmarried mothers.

The bleak future facing the unmarried mother with little legal redress must have exercised a great restraining influence on many girls, aside from religious or family considerations. Her whole future was generally blighted. Even if her father was willing to settle a larger dowry than normal on her, she would have felt that it was the dowry which inspired the prospective husband to marry her, not love or affection. The grim lives lived by these girls is seen in the following words: 'The woman that is guilty of the offence is slighted and shunned by all her former acquaintances. It is remembered against the grandchild and is often reproached to her family for twenty years. There is a great reluctance to marry such a person, but in the poverty of this country a small sum of money forms a great temptation and is often yielded to.'[16] If the girl had no money or dowry, her chances were almost inevitably ruined, particularly as marriage was the aim of most young girls.

Yet even within the County, the treatment of the unmarried mother varied from parish to parish, as is clear from the answers of the Parish priests to the Poverty Commission, 1835. There was a sad lack of responsibility on the part of the fathers evident in some parishes, such as Ballintubber. An irate Rev. John Kirby

---

[16] Ibid. Evidence of Rev. Fr. Waldron, p. 52.

27. Inniskea Islands, off the Mullet Peninsula, with many old religious traditions and customs, had many evictions and much depopulation in this period.

wrote as follows: 'I have baptized seventeen bastard children whose parents are destitute, mostly servants. The fathers do not contribute in the least to their support.'[17] While the number of unmarried mothers was not as great in Ballinrobe, eight as against seventeen in Ballintubber, a similar picture of irresponsibility presented itself.[18] In Kilmina, mothers supported their children by begging.[19] In Islandeady, while some of the children were supported by the mother's begging, others were supported by the mother of the reputed father.[20] In Killasser, where there were few illegitimate children in the parish, these were supported by the reputed fathers.[21]

---

[17] Supplement to Appendix A, p. 21.
[18] Ibid., p. 26.
[19] Ibid. Evidence of Rev. Mr. Sheridan, p. 21.
[20] Ibid. Evidence of Rev. Peter Ward, p. 21.
[21] Ibid. Evidence of Rev. John McNulty, p. 26.

One is not surprised that the position in which these girls found themselves caused a few of them to commit crime. I have found no evidence of abortion, but there were a few cases of infanticide, in which the children were invariably believed to be illegitimate. In one case the mother was turned out of doors by her parents, partly for the disgrace she brought on them, partly from their inability to support an increase in family. Under these circumstances and unable to support the child by her own industry, she was driven to the commission of crime.[22] One suspects that some cases of desertion were committed by unmarried mothers driven to desperation, but the evidence is vague as such cases were notoriously difficult to prove in Court. It is also possible that in the days before mandatory postmortems after suspicious deaths that a far higher rate of infanticide and death by desertion was a reality. One also wonders if some respondents wished to present their own area in the best possible light. In Islandeady, the Parish priest spoke of thirteen such mothers. Theobald Burke[23] who did not know of any in the same parish, wrote: 'I am proud to say immorality on the part of females is scarcely known here'. To be fair, however, the Parish Priest had a much more practical knowledge of the matter.

Irrespective of location, however, the lot of an unmarried mother was very difficult and probably became more difficult as time progressed, particularly during the harsh years of the Famine, when people's hearts hardened on occasions in a grim struggle for survival, and when the widow with young children was much more likely to receive support when begging than an unmarried mother.

---

[22] Appendix A, p. 4.
[23] Supplement to Appendix A. Evidence of Rev. Peter Ward and Theobald Burke, p. 2.

9

Widows

Unlike the unmarried mother, widows were highly esteemed by society, however, most lived lives of abject misery, once called virtuous poverty.

Very few of them were well provided for by their husbands, but this does not necessarily imply neglect on their part. Servants or cattle jobbers might sometimes lay up some provision for them but a laborer could not do so.[1] As a result, many laborers' widows surrendered their houses on their husbands' deaths, if the husbands held such and resorted to begging.[2] However, this did not mark a great change for many of them, as most laborers' wives and families were accustomed to beg when laborers were out of employment.[3] Many widows were rendered homeless by illness, as cabins were often destroyed after death by cholera.[4]

The fortunes of widows with land varied considerably. In some instances, where people held land in joint tenancies, the other tenants insisted on widows leaving the tenancies, lest they might be unable to pay the rent. The case of the Widow M'Intire reveals the plight of such widows. She and her two children were living by begging in 1836. Her husband had died a few weeks previously. He held land under a joint lease which the other tenants would not suffer her to continue to hold lest she should fall into arrears for which they would be accountable.[5]

Many widows, unless they inherited considerable substance as well as land, gradually sank into beggary. This was often the case

[1]   Appendix A, p. 123.
[2]   Ibid. Evidence of John Duffey, Ardnaree, p. 122.
[3]   Ibid. Evidence of John Duffey, p. 122.
[4]   Ibid. Evidence of Widow Reily, p. 126.
[5]   Ibid., p. 298.

with widows whose children were too young either to help them on the land or contribute in some way to the family income. The Widow McCoy in Burrishoole illustrates this process. She set as much land as paid the rent and reserved the remainder planting it with potatoes. While appearing more prosperous than some of her neighbors, she had but a single fold of a blanket for her whole family and was often without straw for bedding. She was cited as a case of a lady sinking into beggary.[6]

The treatment of widows by landlords depended on the whim of the landlord. To aggravate matters, there was no public support for widows, from which they could derive financial support.[7] In general, when a man died and left no substance the widow was deprived of her land in a most unmerciful manner. One bailiff stated: 'I have deprived a great number of widows myself of their holdings; I *canted* (sold off) all they had in the world, except that I did not meddle with the blanket, that was not worth putting keepers on; or I might in charity leave them a few barrels of their potatoes, that they might not starve when they are put out from the house and land'.[8]

Few landlords helped the widows of deceased tenants; these were landlords who knew the country intimately. Absentee landlords did nothing to help. Describing a more humane and kindly landlord, one witness said: 'There are a few decent widows, whose husbands were tenants to Major Bingham that he has taken pity on and given each a cabin and a small spot of ground rent-free that keeps them from beggary. It is not a general rule with him to do so; he could not support all the poverty on his estate; his entire rent roll would not be enough for that; no other landlord in the parish (Kilmore Erris) does even so much; and the other landlords are either absentees, or have not the property to afford to give such assistance'.[9] Another landlord who helped was Captain Steward in Burrishoole[10] who

---

6   Ibid., p. 123.
7   Ibid., p. 124.
8   Ibid., p. 125.
9   Ibid. Evidence of James Donoghue, p. 125.
10   Ibid., p. 123.

28. Knox Street, later renamed Pearse Street, Ballina.

gave casual help and also half an acre rent free to such widows. In this parish, there was also a bequest from a Lady O'Donnel of £15 per annum, distributed among the parish poor, half by the Protestant clergyman and the other half by the Catholic clergyman.[11] In Aughavale, there was a private place for 6 widows supported by subscription.[12] One landlord's agent asserted that a widow and orphans would get more indulgence from

---

[11] Ibid., p. 123.
[12] Appendix E. Evidence of Rev. R. Creighton, p. 126.

their landlords than other tenants; in Westport, many widows obviously made great efforts to retain their miserable hovels. This agent found widows and orphans more punctual in paying their rents than Lord Sligo's other tenantry.[13]

For widows who held on to their land, there was great support forthcoming both from neighbors and usually from relations. Tillage was done for them gratuitously and laborers very commonly worked for them on holidays and on Sunday mornings.[14] Relatives and neighbors were very ready to help them, though unable to undertake their whole support. They often supported them by taking charge of one or their children. Very few widows who held on to their land had sufficiency of either food or clothing. A widow in Aughavale who had set part of her land at profit rent and laboring in the field herself 'is by this means enabled to hire some assistance, requiring no gratuitous labor. This supports her and her family but does not half support her'. In this parish, including the town of Westport, only one widow derived support for herself and family from means other than land, being employed and receiving 4d. a day at a small neighborhood cotton factory, the only establishment of its kind in this province.

Widows, such as the Widow Kilboy, worked and lived in a 'most laborious and wretched manner'. This gallant lady was employed to tend oats in the process of kiln-drying. 'I am obliged for this purpose to watch it, without intermission, for twenty four hours, remaining up during the whole night and am paid from 7d., to 4d. for each kiln cast, according as the business may be pressing or slack. The most I could attend to is four kiln-casts in the week.'[15] This lady earned at most 2s. 6d. per week. It was little wonder that she stated that most beggars lived better than she and her family, as she was often obliged to live on a meal of dry potatoes in times of scarcity; she had been unable to buy clothes for them for a year. Some resorted to dealing in illicit whiskey, a more profitable business than any other.

---

[13] Appendix A. Evidence of Mr. Large, p. 121.
[14] Ibid. Evidence of Mr. M'Nally, p. 121.
[15] Ibid., p. 125.

29. Enniscoe House, Crossmolina, Co. Mayo.

Generally, widows with young children had to beg to support them, but on other occasions were forced to do so to pay local taxes. In one case, villagers threatened to seize a widow's blanket to pay the county cess.[16] The fact that she had young children aided the widow to obtain charity but it mitigated against her chances of obtaining employment. 'There is a widow in my village with five or six children that would not get work, if she gave her labor for her food; the children would be following her and one would have the support of them for he (the employer) could not refuse them a meal'.[17] This feeling was widespread. In

[16] Ibid., p. 123.
[17] Ibid. Evidence of William Butler, Cong, p. 124.

the Westport area, there were at least 100 widows supported by begging[18] and in the Castlebar area there were 61 widows with 100 children in a similar position.[19]

In general, widows were very unwilling to beg on losing their land and they endeavored to secure a corner in a neighbor's house, either by way of charity, or on the promise of paying some trifle for it.[20] Many widows who depended greatly on the help and charity of friends and neighbors at home resorted to begging in times of scarcity.[21] In many cases, rather than shame their people, they left home by night and went into a distant part of the country and, having begged for three or four months, when plenty came back, they returned to shift among their friends again.

Widows who had older children sometimes fared better,[22] but one also reads of widows supporting children or in-laws out of work.[23] Some widows, at one time self-supporting, had to beg owing to changed family circumstances. Catherine Flynn did not beg until she was left with the care of five young grandchildren, whose parents had died of cholera.[24] Some widows may have received support in some areas from the Church Poor List. Ballinrobe usually had 30 widows on this list.[25]

Sometimes, widows who had a house and furniture tried to support themselves by opening feeding houses, letting beds, etc. to travelers and beggars.[26] This often occurred in towns and villages, because no charge was usually made for lodgings to beggars in the country. In Kilmaine, the usual rate was 2d. per night for an individual traveler, and a poor family might be accommodated for 6d. to 8d. per night.

---

[18] Supplement to Appendix A, p. 21.
[19] Appendix A, p. 125.
[20] Ibid. Evidence of Rev. Richard Gibbons, p. 29.
[21] Ibid., p. 125.
[22] Supplement to Appendix A, p. 30, reference to Crossboyne.
[23] Appendix A. Derrygarriff, p. 499.
[24] Ibid., p. 496.
[25] Supplement to Appendix A. Evidence of Rev. Thomas J. Burke, p. 26.
[26] Appendix A, p. 120.

Some interesting facts are revealed by comparing the population figures for 1841 with those of 1851. In every Barony, in 1841, there were more male heads of families, 170,140 as against 161,632 female.[27] In 1851, there were 112,141 female heads of families and 111,354 male. There were more female heads of families in seven of the nine county baronies. The exceptions were Clanmorris and Costello. Many of these female heads of families were widows and an increased number of deserted wives. The incidence of widowhood by barony shows some surprising facts. In Murrisk, widows comprised 25.27% of the total female population, followed by Erris with 20.7% and Kilmaine with 19.02%. By contrast, widows comprised 8.2% of the total female population of Costello.[28] Thus there were 3.08 times as many widows in Murrisk as in Costello. Many references were made to cholera widows, as cholera killed young men in particular.

The breakdown of figures for the Barony of Tirawley, parish by parish, is interesting. Moygownagh had an equal number of male and female heads of families. Kilbride and Kilmoremoy each had fewer women heads of households. All other parishes of the Barony had more females than males as heads of households, especially Kilfian parish, which had 1,470 female and 1,248 male heads of households, a difference of 122.

Many of these female heads of households were widows.[29] The 1851 Census reveals that Moygownagh, with an equal number of female and male heads, had a very large number of widows, 17.7% of the total female population, followed by Doonfeeney with 13.69% and Ballycastle town with 12.56%. Templemurray had the least number with 7.9% of the total female population.

The fact that a third of widows in the County, as in County Galway, were in public institutions in 1851 speaks for itself.

---

[27] Census 1841 – General Tables, p. 400. Table I.
[28] Census 1851, p. 574.
[29] Ibid., Widows in Tirawley, p. 574.

30. Wedding party outside Scoil Acla on Achill Island in 1911. It includes Emily Weddall, a founder of Scoil Acla in 1910, noted for its contribution to the Irish language, music and culture.

10

Religion

The term 'hidden Catholicism' often applied to Catholicism in Ireland in the seventeenth and eighteenth centuries could also be applied to particular aspects of Irish Catholicism in the nineteenth century.

There is a dearth of information with regard to certain aspects of religious practice, and thus one is left with an impressionistic picture of this practice which was an integral part of the lives of so many people.

While told that people had 'a strong and living enthusiasm for religion',[1] one wonders about Mass attendance, which is central to Catholic belief. The earliest available figures for the country as a whole date from 1834. Miller[2] concluded, on the basis of sampling areas which seemed firmest, that attendance in rural English-speaking areas ranged from 30% to 60% and the rural Irish-speaking areas at 20% to 40%. He qualified this conclusion by stating that he was not conducting a socio-religious study and the figures available could be interpreted in several ways. This seems a very low figure, but no allowance was made for those not bound to hear Mass, especially children under 7, whose attendance was frowned on rather than approved of, if they distracted the congregation. The sixth of a set of rules published for 'Conduct in the house of God' reads as follows: 'Mothers should take care not to disturb the congregation by bringing children under the age required.'[3] Another expert

---

[1] Tocqueville, Alexis de, *Journeys*: Reply from a P.P. cited in Kerr, D. *Peel, Priests and Politics*, p. 191.

[2] Miller, D., 'Irish Catholicism and The Great Famine' in Journal of Social History' (ix) (1975), pp. 81–98.

[3] Catholic Directory 1836. Rules for Conduct in the House of God

[129]

reckoned that one-fifth of the total population did not come to Mass, because they were not bound to. These included the aged, the sick and mothers minding small children. He concludes that there was effective 100% attendance at Mass in the towns; in the rural English-speaking areas, 37.5% to 75%; in the rural Irish-speaking areas, 25% to 50%. These are, of course, minimum figures.[4] There is no reason to believe that Mass attendance in Mayo differed from the national pattern.

Very important in the lives of many women may have been the 'Stations' (*see* Note) held in farmhouses in different parts of the parish, which 'gave more people the opportunity of attending Mass and receiving the Sacraments.'[5] Many people hold that some people did not attend Sunday Mass because they had neither proper clothing nor shoes, a shortage more readily remedied at the Stations, where one good cloak and gown in a village might serve to have women well dressed, when they went to Confession at Station Masses. A Parish Priest describes women changing a cloak and gown after they left Confession, and giving it to the next woman to make her appear respectable.[6]

After Mass came devotion to Our Lady, especially the Rosary. This was followed by many traditional Irish devotions such as 'Patterns' (*see* Note), pilgrimages, holy wells which combined religion with celebration. The Irish Bishops in 1829 expressed their fears 'lest the superstitious excessive festivity of many of those practices prevail over their religious aspects and lead to abuses.'[7] Yet they continued unabated in Mayo. The great pilgrimage to Croagh Patrick near Murrisk was very popular. Patterns still continued at places such as Kilcummin[8] where 5 patterns yearly were held at St. Cummin's well. While local tradition maintains that these sometimes led to faction fights,

quoted in Patrick J. Corish, *The Catholic Community in the eighteenth and nineteenth centuries* Helicon Press, 1981, p. 507.

4   Corish, Patrick J., op. cit. p. 107.
5   Kerr, D., *Peel, Priests and Politics*, p. 48.
6   Appendix A. Evidence of Rev. Mr. Gibbons, p. 372.
7   Meeting of Irish Bishops. D.D.A., 11th February, 1829.
8   O.S. Field Books: Mayo, p. 1277.

31. After Mass political meeting at Lahardane in the second half of the 19th century. People are dressed in their Sunday best. In the midst of the crowd, a constable listens attentively.

one can imagine the enjoyment these patterns brought to the lives of women, who met all their friends and enjoyed the festivities. Prayers at Holy Wells were very common; there was a strong belief in the curative power of water from these wells. Stations were held at least up to the year 1833 at Toberkeeran Holy Well in Addergoole Parish.[9] There was great local devotion at other holy wells such as St. Patrick's Well at Leigue (Ballina), at Downpatrick on Garland Sunday (last Sunday of July), St. Brigid's Well at Ratheskin and the Holy Well in Doonfeeney (St. Dervla).

---

9   Ibid., p. 19.

Religion was a dominant force in women's lives at the major events of births, marriages and deaths. Women were generally very anxious to have their babies baptized very soon after birth on account of the belief in Limbo. As well as that, many a distressed mother suffered greatly at the thought of her unbaptized child being buried in unconsecrated ground, in special graveyards which were reserved for still-born and unbaptized children, such as those at Tonybaun[10] and Glandawoo.[11] The registers show that Baptisms were only delayed in the cases of the children of mixed marriages, who were sometimes baptized 'after the Parson.'

Women played a minor role in the actual Church services, including Baptism; it was usual to have one male and female sponsor for each child baptized. The Kilfian Register lists four Baptisms with men sponsors only, 3 Baptisms where one woman sponsor only was listed. In Crossmolina, the usual pattern of sponsorship applied, though there are two Baptisms recorded where one male sponsor and two women sponsors were listed. The Foxford Register, which really comes after the period under consideration, has 9 Baptisms in its early years, for which no sponsors whatever are listed. We know that Churching after birth was very important in women's lives. The Knockmore Parish Register unusually records both Churchings and Baptisms.

Most marriages took place in Church, or sometimes in the house where the young couple were to live. Church rules governing marriage within the degrees of kindred were strictly enforced; one reads in the Crossmolina Register of two sets of first cousins marrying by special dispensation. This dispensation was not always forthcoming and one couple, not in receipt of the special dispensation, were married in Kilfian by a 'discarded priest' silenced because of his alcoholism. One suspects that one couple married in Crossmolina by such a priest were described in the Crossmolina Register as 'illegitimate parents',

---

[10] Ibid., p. 514.
[11] Ibid., p. 340.

first cousins who had gone through a form of marriage without special dispensation. Few widows remarried, including one in Crossmolina parish and three widowers, one a stonemason aged seventy five. Parish priests were concerned about the validity of marriages in rape cases. A man accused of rape often married the girl who brought the charge against him, to avoid either being hanged or transported. The charge of rape was often dropped on the occasion of marriage, the so-called 'out-of-dock marriages'. Dean Lyons was convinced that nine out of ten of these cases was an attempt to coerce an unwilling man into marriage. This abuse became so widespread that Archbishop John MacHale banned the solemnisation of marriage where such cases were pending in the Civil Courts. The deplorable practice of out of dock marriages continued into the second half of the century. Beside an entry for marriage in Crossmolina in 1863 is written: 'settled with clerk-rape up to this date.'

The Famine halted many marriages unless the couples were fairly well off. Unlike earlier years where one sometimes saw the abbreviations N.P. besides an entry for marriage, all marriage dues for Crossmolina were paid for in this year, which would suggest that the very poor did not marry during this year. By contrast the year 1833 had three marriages recorded with the notation N.P. written beside them.

Over the years, many people may have been unable to pay marriage dues. The Parish Priest of Crossmolina was owed £4. 18. 0. for marriages in 1832. Several entries for marriage dues paid by instalment occur. Wedding dues were a guinea in the year 1839, a not inconsiderable sum for some. Not even priests were immune from bad debts, however; in 1846 one entry reads 'one case of contracting parties who fled about a year since, not paid.'

Not all marriage situations were regular. The Crossmolina Register reveals various living arrangements. Cases of bigamy occurred. One couple lived together for twenty years before getting married. One is not told why they waited so long to get married. Another man had deserted his wife and set up another household in the area. One couple were separated – 'the husband's fault' according to the Register. Another was living apart, because of poverty. Kilfian seems to have adhered to the rule of no marriages in Lent and Advent, a rule less strictly adhered to in Crossmolina. All weddings in both parishes had one woman witness and one male witness. This also applied to the later parish Register of Foxford. Active participation by women in church services was confined to sponsorship at Baptism and acting as witnesses at weddings. Women did not fare much better in the other churches. There were no women Ministers of Religion of other denominations in 1851, but there were three lady sextons.

Of particular interest is the work done by the Sisters of Mercy in Ballina at the end of this period. Forbes described their work in glowing terms. These sisters spent their time 'educating the young, nursing, feeding the hungry, clothing the naked and harboring the homeless.'[12] Of particular interest is their work in the Temperance Movement, started in the town earlier but which had fallen into decline. 'They have added a full hundred to the old remnants, and are zealously and successfully following up their triumph. Their plan is to accept pledges, at first for a period of twelve months only, finding it much more easy to obtain them for that limited period; and well-judging that the great majority of those who have kept the pledge for that period will renew it permanently.' The success of the movement in Ballina was due to their zeal. He continued: 'They are found to exercise a much greater supervision over their pledged clients than any other persons could do and proportional results may be expected from their labours.'[13]

Women of other religious denominations had long taken an active part in education in the County. In 1826,[14] there were 23 Catholic female teachers in the County, sixteen Protestant and two whose religion was not stated. Many of these saw the

---

12 Forbes, John, *Memorandums*, p. 28.
13 Forbes, John, Ibid., p. 26.
14 Appendix 22 – Parochial Returns: Appendix to the Second Report from the Commissioners of Irish Educational Inquiry Vol. XL.

32. The interior of a forge in the Newport. Blacksmiths played an important role in rural areas.

need for providing what the Quakers called 'permanent relief' – work and training for work. A case in point was the Presbyterian School in Ballina town, an industrial school in its best sense, in which all, except 6 of its pupils, were Catholics. 'No bribes in the way of food or clothing are held out to the Catholics to attend it; but the girls receive the profit on their own work and obtain all the materials at a cheaper rate.'[15] Such philanthropy also marked the schools set up by the Belfast Ladies Industrial Association for Connaught in co-operation with the Society of Friends.

As the period progressed, a sinister element entered the situation. There were some attempts made at proselytism, commonly called Souperism in the area, which caused much anguish and anger and often caused members of the Protestant

---

[15]   Forbes, John, op. cit. p. 17.

Churches to be indiscriminately branded as Soupers. The cause of militant Protestantism received a great boost when the fanatically evangelical Thomas Plunket was appointed Protestant Archbishop of Tuam. His sister, Catherine Plunket, involved in a notorious episode of Souperism in the Lough Mask area, had set up a school. Tales about her encouragement of proselytism and Souperism abounded in the area. She was more powerful than most evangelical women because of her family connections, including the support of her powerful brother for the Irish Church Missions.

The Belmullet area was scourged by efforts at proselytism carried out by a few men and women of various religious groups, particularly during the Famine. This area was regarded by such people as promising because of poverty, reprehensible landlords and poor relief organization. John Lees took an active part in conversion work, when he came to the area. In this, he was helped by three curates paid by the Irish Society and assisted by his wife, Lady Louisa, who ran a convert school in Belmullet.[16] However, they seem to have confined their efforts at conversion to the school. They did not make a change of religion a condition of giving Famine relief which occupied much of their time, otherwise they would not have been appointed by the Quakers in the distribution of relief. Others were not so scrupulous. Fr. Reilly of Bangor and Ballycroy wrote to his friend, Thomas Synott, of what was happening in Erris. 'Another of our grievances and not the least, is the existence of proselytizing schools where famishing children are allowed daily a half pound of meal as the price of their apostasy, and the fact is, that many even advanced in years have been seduced by starvation to wear the external garb of a foreign faith, who in all probability would willingly meet the scaffold in support of their own – their ancient faith – but death by famine is even more trying than that of the scaffold. Of these unfortunate schools, I have in my parish a few of Mr. Nangle's creation. This is their hour and well they avail themselves of it, not to relieve the poor, but to rob them of what

---

[16]   Bowen, D., *Souperism, Myth or Reality*, p. 194.

is and ought to be dearer than life.'[17] Further along the coast at Doonfeeney, Rev. Fr. Hart, who worked well with Protestant ministers for relief work, was driven to complain about the 'proselytising agents from different societies with plenty of meal money,' who were active in his parish.[18]

There is no doubt that proselytism took place, though it is hard to quantify it. This is particularly clear when we see it being condemned by both Protestant Ministers and lay Protestants. Even the mild-spoken Forbes wished people to be very clear about the differences between 'the ordinary schools so liberally provided by the Presbyterian Church and the Missions Schools new to the ultimate conversion of the Roman Catholics.'[19] It is equally clear that some women took part in this campaign of Souperism.

How far did religion influence the lives of women? Archbishop John MacHale spoke of the great 'influence exercised by religion on the Irish peasantry.'[20] This, I think, is particularly so in the case of women. Religion certainly combined with social and economic factors to keep the number of unmarried mothers at a much lower level than in European countries. It may have been a strong influence in keeping women from being involved in much serious crime.

On occasion, priests connived with women to break the civil law, with particular reference to poteen making, which employed several industrious women. Many priests were probably unselfish in this support but it was also stated that 'the clergy's due and tithes like the landlord's rent were swollen by the trade in poteen.'[21] A good still represented a large investment for very poor men and women and it was alleged that an Achill friar

---

[17] Reilly, Fr. Patrick: Letter to Thomas Synnott of the Central Relief Committee, 15th March 1849 – D.D.A. Fol. 1001 Archbishop Murray's Correspondence.

[18] Hart, Fr. Martin: Letter to Thomas Synnott, January 1848. Archdiocesan Archives, Dublin Mss. 1005, 25th January 1848.

[19] Forbes, John, Op. cit. p. 17.

[20] Appendix A, p. 120. Evidence of Archbishop John McHale.

[21] Otway, Caesar: *Sketches in Erris and Tirawley*, Dublin 1841, p. 361.

earned the greater part of his living by blessing illicit stills.[22] Many a poor woman may have felt that such a blessing afforded protection against the Revenue authorities and a hope of a steady income. In these circumstances, one would have expected to hear of much drunkenness among women but this was not the case. A 'woman is hardly ever drunk.'[23] The temptation must have been great for many women, but the influence of religion, poverty and social strictures acted as restraining influences.

There is no doubt that religion was very important in women's lives. Belief in God sustained them in the difficult lives which they led. Devotion to Our Lady and locally revered Saints made religion a very personal experience for them. Women were anxious about religious observance such as Mass attendance and reception of the Sacraments of Baptism, Marriage and the Last Rites. As well as efforts to influence their religious beliefs by proselytizing agents, their faith was also sorely tested on occasions by the behavior of some priests. In the 19th century, their faith did not blind people to the vices exhibited by some priests, mainly drunkenness, women and avarice. They showed remarkable understanding and tolerance of every clerical vice, except avarice.[24] Quite revealing is the petition to the Pope from

---

[22] Noel, B.W., *A Short Tour Through the Midlands of Ireland* 1836 (1837), p. 19.

[23] Appendix E. Evidence of Rev. Mr. Dwyer and R. M'Manus, p. 102.

[24] Larkin, Emmett: 'The Devotional Revolution in Ireland, 1850–1979' in *American Historical Review* 77 *(1972)*

For fuller details on a very troubled history, Brendan Hoban's book, Turbulent Diocese The Killala Diocese, 1798–1848 is particularly useful. p. 339 etc.

Note 1: *'Stations'* The custom of the *'Stations'* or *'Station Masses'* developed as a reaction to the Penal Laws in Ireland. They represented the adaptation of the Catholic population to the Draconian Laws, known as the Penal Laws enacted between 1697 and 1746, which were on the statute book for many years thereafter.

Among the religious provisions was a ban on Mass, the destruction of Catholic places of worship, (although some were taken over and used as Protestant Churches) and an outright ban on Catholic clergy, who were regarded as traitors who, if caught, could be sentenced to death. Many priests operated under different disguises. (Presbyterians who were also subject to the Penal Laws found them very restrictive, although they

the parishioners of Kilcommen Erris in 1840, which contained 15 heads of complaint which show the sufferings and humiliation endured by poor parishioners caused by the 'avaricious ire' of a difficult priest; these were not isolated incidents.[25] The fact that most kept their faith is a tribute to the strength of that faith, as they would have expected better from a Catholic priest. While

---

do not seem to have been enforced as strictly in their case). However, the Catholic population generally remained loyal to the priests and to the Mass. Two new traditions developed: the tradition of the Mass Rock and the *Stations*. Mass was often celebrated on a given rock, often on high ground, which gave a vantage point to the congregation to ward off surprise attacks by the military. Mass was celebrated by priests in disguise. Mass kits were stored carefully by members of the congregation. The sites of Mass rocks are still regarded as sacred. One of the most famous rocks in Mayo is the Keem Bay Mass Rock on Achill Island.

Masses were also said in people's houses or cabins, known as the *Stations* because of the random nature of the houses selected. With the relaxation over time of the Penal Laws and particularly after the granting of Catholic Emancipation in 1829, churches began to be built, although this occurred very slowly in some districts, because of the lack of funds available. The tradition of the *Stations* continued. They were very popular, having both religious and social elements, where hospitality was extended to priests and people in attendance at the Station House. The tradition still lives in some parishes. *Station* Masses were especially valued by members of the faith who could not attend Mass on the grounds of age, infirmity, distance from church, lack of suitable transport and the welcome extended to neighbors was an integral part of the *Station*. Before the broadcasting of Mass on Radio, or the transmission of Mass on Television and other electronic media, the *Stations* were the only means for some people to hear Mass.

Note 2: *Patterns*: The word derives from the Irish '*Patrún*' or patron Saint, which each parish had in earlier times. Saints' Days or Patterns were frequently celebrated around Holy Wells. The Synod of Tuam (1660) attempted to limit them because of irreligious and licentious behavior associated with them, while acknowledging the religious devotions which they inspired and people's belief in the curative powers of the holy water from these wells. The Penal Laws also affected them adversely. The Act to prevent the Further Growth of Popery had a limited effect on them, as it was largely ignored by the landlords tasked to enforce it. However, it was the Great Famine which sounded the death knell of the custom, with a few exceptions. Their passing was mourned by Sir Wm. Wilde in '*Popular Irish Superstitions*' (1849). (This note is based on information provided by *inter alia* Kevin Danaher in *The Year in Ireland*).

[25] Ibid.

some women accepted the blandishments of Soupers, sometimes for brief periods, this should not lead us to believe that they had lost their Faith, as many of these women, half-crazed by the Famine, were willing to go to any lengths to preserve the lives of their children and would accept any external condition to get food. Most of them reverted to their old faith when the crisis has passed. Such a crisis also caused several parents and teachers to become overzealous with regard to the teaching of religion, attempting to ensure that young people would not stray from their faith. In that regard, the advice from the influential Catholic Bishop J.K.L. (Dr James Doyle, Bishop of Kildare and Leighlin) who promoted sound educational practices is illuminating:

> 'Be always lenient to the children and not angry, even with the perverse. Do not hope to make them all good and do not require the practice of much piety from any of them, lest the yoke of religion become heavy to them. Rather permit and encourage the devotion of those of them whom Nature may dispose to be fervent. In all things, have a firm reliance on God', cited in the Thesis 'Phases of Education in Galway in the Nineteenth Century'
> by K.P. Hackett (1937) U.C.G.

While fanatical Religion led in some cases to men and women regarding the Famine as a God-sent opportunity to produce conversions to their own brand of Faith by fair means or foul, a strong religious belief led to the quiet heroism shown by women of all religious persuasions in their practical efforts to alleviate hunger and want during the great tragedy of the Famine and the lean years which followed, often at great personal cost, sometimes at the cost of their lives. Only lives rooted in faith and anchored to strong religious beliefs could have sustained the sufferings of the Famine and the philanthropic attempts to relieve suffering humanity, at a time when self-preservation would have seemed the most sensible course of action.

I I

Crime

The low incidence of crime among women is clear when one examines the available evidence, though the crime rate increased dramatically in the period under consideration.

Jail returns are fascinating. For instance, in 1826, there was no female in Castlebar jail.[1] By 1841, there were 10,085 males and 1,763 females in the Hospitals attached to jails in Mayo. Males outnumbered females by almost six to one. Of these inmates 9 males and 2 females died. Francis White, the Inspector of Jails, reported that in 1845, there was one female and twelve men for trial at Assizes. At this time, nobody either male or female was under sentence of death.[2] By 1851, women comprised one quarter of the prison population in Castlebar jail[3], and in the Bridewell (small town jail) of this town were an equal number of men and women. Three women were detained in Swinford Bridewell and 5 women in Ballina Bridewell. The over-all figures for the County reveal that there were 9 women in jail in 1851 as against 281 males.

The crimes for which women were committed to prison were generally very petty. Assizes Reports in the Mayo Constitution of July 1828 make interesting reading. Two ladies, Catherine Hickey and Judith Powel, were charged with feloniously stealing a pair of trousers from a stall in Westport on market day. The jury found Judith Powel guilty, as she had taken them under her

---

[1]   Appendix No.12, British Parliamentary Papers, Volume 40, p. 156.
[2]   British Parliamentary Papers, Volume 2, Session 1834. Report upon the Table of Deaths 1841, Table LVI.
[3]   Report of Francis White, Inspector of Jails: *Mayo Constitution* November 25th, 1844.

cloak. At the same Assizes, Mary McGowan was charged with stealing silk handkerchiefs in Castlebar. The method employed in the theft revealed a certain ingenuity. The accused introduced a piece of wire with a hook at the end of it between the rails of the shop window and was in the act of putting her hand towards them when the witness (Robert Smith) who was in the far end of the shop observed her and took her into custody.[4]

Thefts of clothing figured in many cases, as in the case of the larceny of an apron in Ballinrobe, in June 1844. In many cases, servants were suspect, unless they attempted to prove their innocence, as shown in the evidence of Mary Staunton, a servant, in the case brought against James Staunton in July 1828. A coat was lost, the possession of D. Doig, Esq., and Mary Thomas found the coat in Mr. Staunton's house. She stated that the coat was remade when she found it 3 days later. She stated that, if she did not prosecute somebody for the theft, her master would charge her with it. A verdict of Not Guilty was recorded in this case.

Thefts of fowl provided causes for litigation; John and Winifred Carney in 1828 were indicted with stealing 5 geese, the goods of Michael Walsh and 6 geese, the property of Mary Rogers. Once again, the jury recorded a Not Guilty verdict.[5]

Occasionally, as at the Mayo Assizes of March 19, 1844, we read of counterfeiting. Judith Flood was indicted for uttering a base half crown at Killala and found guilty.[6]

Many women were charged either singly or jointly with assault. At the Castlebar Petty Sessions of 1844, Constable Connaught[7] brought forward Ellen Murphy, Michael Mulldowney and Sally Fall. The two ladies had allegedly assaulted Mulldowney who had been robbed of five shillings and a handkerchief. Mulldowney's property was found on Murphy, which seemed to indicate guilt.

---

4 Census 1851, Table XI, p. xxi.
5 *Mayo Constitution* July 28th, 1828.
6 Ibid., March 19th, 1844.
7 Report of Castlebar Petty Sessions. *Mayo Constitution* 20th May, 1944.

Some cases tried at the Petty Sessions seem very trivial, but are understandable when one remembers the cramped living quarters, the close proximity of the cabins to each other, and jangled nerves caused by the unremitting struggle against poverty and worsening circumstances. Examples of such cases occurred at Castlebar and Westport. In May, 1844, Margaret Davidson was charged with attacking her two neighbors,[8] who had driven her husband's cow to pound for trespass. A regular form of insult figured at the Westport Petty Sessions in June 1844, when the a lady was charged with throwing water into her opponent's face.[9]

Fractious tempers among inmates of institutions led to charges being preferred, as at Castlebar in March 1845.[10] A Mrs. Bingham, an inmate of Castlebar Workhouse, complained that she had been assaulted by another female pauper called Brennan. Mrs Bingham had been employed by the Matron to supervise the wash. Part of this duty consisted of taking clothes from other inmates. A derogatory comment passed on Brennan's clothing led to the attack, which may also reflect resentment of another inmate having been promoted to a position of authority, however lowly, and perhaps a less than tactful use of this authority on the part of the plaintiff.

Not all charges brought against women were so trivial. There were occasional convictions for manslaughter. Ellen McGiven and Bridget Dolan were sentenced to 3 months hard labor for manslaughter at the Spring Assizes of 1846.[11] Occasionally, women were charged with murder. At the Ballinrobe Quarter Sessions of 1844,[12] Sarah Flynn was indicted for the murder of a female child named Mary Flynn by throwing her into a river at Esker and was charged with having killed the child by drowning. The accused was acquitted of the charge on a technicality. The

---

8   Ibid., May 20th, 1844.
9   Ibid., June 23rd, 1844.
10 Ibid., Report of the Petty Sessions, March 18th, 1845.
11 Ibid., Report of the Spring Assizes, March 20th, 1946.
12 Ibid., Report of the Quarter Sessions, June 23rd, 1844.

jury would have found her guilty, had the indictment charged her with first having suffocated the child and then thrown her into the water.

There were also rare charges of child desertion, notoriously difficult to prove, which were generally dismissed through lack of evidence. A rare case of conviction for this offence was that of Mary Thomas – sentenced to 6 months imprisonment in 1847.[13] It was somewhat easier to secure conviction in the few cases of infanticide. These provide an interesting insight into the social climate of the time, with its rather unbending rigid attitudes towards unmarried mothers and the failure of the alleged fathers to provide support. Generally, these cases were occasioned by lack of support from the girl's family and the children were invariably illegitimate. In one parish, there were 2 cases of infanticide in two years, both reputed to have been caused by the father's refusal to support the child. In one of these cases, the mother was turned out of doors by her parents, partly from the disgrace she brought on the family, partly from their inability to support an increase in family; under these circumstances, and unable to support the child by her own industry, she was driven to the commission of the crime.[14]

Such crimes as murder, manslaughter, or infanticide were regarded as social crimes; those found guilty of them, or believed to be guilty of them, generally faced opprobrium and social condemnation. This stigma also applied to theft. No such stigma, however, attached to offences such as selling illicit spirits and in 1844,[15] we learn from Francis White that there were 7 females and 14 males in jail for their involvement in illicit distillation. There was also a rather indulgent attitude towards those who tried to outwit the law, not only with regard to Revenue duties, but also with regard to claims for Allowances. At the Castlebar Petty Sessions of May 1844,[16] a case was brought by a magistrate

---

13 Ibid., 23rd March 1847.
14 Appendix A, p. 4.
15 Report of Francis White, Inspector of Jails, *Mayo Constitution*, November 25th, 1844.
16 *Mayo Constitution*, 20th May 1844.

against a group of two men and a woman claiming £3 for the support of a deserted child, a child who in fact belonged to one of them. No such approval or indulgence would have been granted to women taking part in organized crime. In 1849, we read of Mr. Corrigan, a farmer in the Westport area, who was robbed of one hundred hides. The police arrested Hoban, the leader of a desperate gang of housebreakers and robbers, and his sister who was a willing accomplice.[17]

The sentences passed on women convicted of crimes reveal an increasing severity, particularly during the Famine years, which may be attributed to the panic felt by the authorities at the 'huge rise in crime.' Harsh sentences were handed down especially for crimes against property, which generally consisted of larceny in the case of women. There was a noticeable lack of consistency in many sentences. At the Mayo Assizes of March 1844,[18] Judith Flood, found guilty of using a forged half-crown at Killala, was sentenced to 6 months in prison. A year later[19] at the same Assizes which convicted Judith Flood, Margaret Sullivan was sentenced to 3 months imprisonment for assault, and a similar sentence was passed on Catherine O'Loughlin, for larceny. A much harsher sentence for larceny was passed on Mary Anne Haslett, who was sentenced to 6 months imprisonment with hard labour at Ballinrobe Quarter Sessions (June 1844)[20] for the larceny of an apron. One is then amazed to read that Mary Togher received a sentence of 4 months with hard labor for sheep stealing in 1845.[21] Not all charges of larceny of animals were treated so lightly; charges against women for stealing animals increased during the Famine years, in spite of the harsh sentences meted out to those found guilty. For example, at the 1847 Spring Assizes, Ellen Curry was charged with sow stealing and Mary and Catherine Mally were charged with and convicted

[17] Ibid., July 10th, 1849.
[18] Ibid., March 19th, 1844.
[19] Ibid., March 18th, 1845.
[20] Ibid., June 23rd, 1844.
[21] Ibid., March 18th, 1845.

of goat stealing.[22] At the Castlebar Petty Sessions of 1845, one poor lady, Sarah McTigue, whose evidence has the ring of truth, was sentenced to one years imprisonment with hard labor for stealing wheat, although 'she had been compelled to do so by poverty.'[23] At the Quarter Sessions of July 1847, Mary Anne D'Arcy was sentenced to 7 years transportation for larceny,[24] though this sentence was commuted to imprisonment. Lesser sentences were passed at the 1849 Assizes, when Ellen Curry was sentenced to four months with hard labor and the Malleys to two months hard labor for goat stealing.[25]

The increasing anxiety of the authorities with regard to lawlessness is reflected in the sentences passed for rioting. At the Mayo Assizes of 1844, Mary Walsh and Bridget Walsh were each fined 1d. for riot.[26] Less than a year later at the Castlebar Petty Sessions, Mary Barrett was sentenced to eighteen months with hard labor for 'riot and affray'.[27] Nevertheless, in spite of the petty crimes which occupied much Court time, most women were law abiding. This is reflected in the numbers of prisoners. In 1851, there were 99 women in gaol in Mayo and 281 men.

What caused women to get involved in crimes, such as larceny which carried such a social stigma? Many, including Dean Lyons, felt it was caused by poverty, that 'their morals are borne down by their wants'.[28] In fact, many women stated in their own defense that they had been driven to the commission of theft by poverty. Others felt that the commission of crime was confined to certain sections of the community. Martin Culkeen stated that there was much less crime among the laborers and poorer sections of the community as they 'have not the spirit to be immoral.'[29] While many women were driven to beg, it is

---

[22] Ibid., March 23rd, 1847.
[23] Ibid., March 18th, 1845.
[24] Ibid., July 13th, 1847.
[25] Ibid., July 26th, 1849.
[26] Ibid., July 30th, 1844.
[27] Ibid., March 18th, 1845.
[28] Appendix A. Evidence of Dean Lyons, p. 506.
[29] Appendix A. Evidence of Martin Culkeen, p. 497.

interesting to note that most depredations were committed 'not by beggars but by persons who are ashamed to beg,' to quote M. Culkeen.

One wonders what prison life was like for women convicts. Some insight into their lives is seen in the evidence of Francis White, the Inspector General of Gaols in Mayo.[30] He stated that 'In the female division, employment is provided for prisoners in spinning, needlework, washing, etc. Elementary instruction in reading and writing is also provided by the Matron as part of her official duties. Figures for female employment in Castlebar Gaol read as follows:

Knitting and Spinning	2
Needlework	4
Washing	2
Prison Duties	12
Unemployed or Sick	8

It was noted that the infirmary of this gaol was kept clean for those who were ill. Conditions were much better than those in most cabins, but much strain may have been occasioned by the fact that mentally ill patients were also kept in prison.

A prison inspector also bemoaned 'the lack of training of prisoners in simple and useful trades, which might with some little sum save them from having the incentive or starvation to disarray them and drive them again into some infringement of the law.' he continued: 'This has happened to many, including a re-committed former prisoner, Ellen M'Navin.' The writer had no doubt that it was the lack of employment opportunities and money either to live on or to set themselves up in some little employment, which mainly contributed to the female crime rate.

Some women were the victims of crime, with attacks of a sexual nature receiving much publicity. At the Castlebar Assizes of 1835, 25 cases of rape were tried;[31] of these, only

---

[30] *Mayo Constitution*, November 25th, 1844.
[31] British Parliamentary Papers, Vol. XLV 1835. Committals (Ireland).

2 were convicted and these men were sentenced to death. At the 1844 Spring Assizes, 5 rape cases were tried.[32] These figures for rape may be exaggerated. Conviction for rape carried the death penalty or transportation and accusations of rape were sometimes made to compel unwilling swains into marriage. Once the promise of marriage was made, these charges were usually withdrawn, even though some girls stated that they intended to make a 'hanging matter' of them. The Mayo Constitution of March 18, 1845 reported the trial of Francis Fitzpatrick who was transported for life for the rape of a young teenager, his wife's first cousin, whom he attacked during his wife's absence from home. Attacks on women were quite common, ranging from common assault to assault with intent to ravish. In 1835, 759 males were convicted in the County. One is amazed that 442 of these convictions were for assault with intent to ravish.[33] There were many cases of assault on women, with an occasional case of murder, such as that of Catherine Hart in 1836.

The Court Records should not blind us to the law-abiding qualities of women in the period under consideration. For example, no woman was convicted in the 1845 Summer Assizes. While many women were charged with petty larceny, one can only be amazed that the figures for this crime were not much higher. The temptation to steal must have been great. On reading the evidence, one cannot but pity the poor women driven by poverty to steal a silk handkerchief or an apron. One feels that women were driven by hunger to steal food such as wheat and potatoes. The motive for stealing geese may not have been so simple. Goose eggs were regarded as a luxury. Geese laid eggs and did not need much care. One suspects that the lady accused of stealing eleven geese before Christmas wished to make a quick profit, perhaps to pay debts or to gain some little sum of cash to enable her to provide herself with some means of employment. Others, such as Mary Anne D'Arcy, may have committed larceny in an attempt to get transported.[34]

---

[32] *Mayo Constitution*, March 12th, 1844.
[33] British Parliamentary Papers. Vol. XLV (Committals).
[34] *Mayo Constitution*, June 8th, 1836.

Many tributes were paid to the honesty of women in the County. Mr. Gildea, whose family had revived the manufacture of coarse linen in Newport and employed between five and six hundred women, left us a glowing account of these women. He stated: 'It is an interesting fact that of 30,000 yards of linen made up to the end of October, 1847 (this work was in progress since January of that year) there is only one piece that was not duly returned to him by the workmen, and he was still hopeful on getting the missing piece.'[35]

Similar tributes were paid to the honesty of the people of Achill. Trevelyan reported that 'The natives of Achill are charged with being thieves and murderers; and if I were to place full reliance of all I heard at the Settlement (the Protestant Mission at Dugort) they would appear to be so. However, Mr. Long who has resided there for many years has never lost even a potato.'[36] Women were regarded as being more honest with regard to paying their debts and rents. This honesty is also reflected in official figures. In 1844, in Castlebar Gaol, there were 8 male master debtors in jail but no female. This, of course, may reflect the small number of women in business and how difficult any of them would have found it to obtain credit.[37]

Did women serve the sentences to which they were condemned? Some did, but many did not, particularly those sentenced to transportation. One may imagine the disappointment of some girls who had committed crime in the hope of being transported, when the sentence for transportation was commuted to imprisonment in an Irish gaol. An examination of the Transportation Registers show that few women, in fact, were sentenced to transportation, one in 1845, 8 in 1847, 13 in 1848 and 2 in 1849. Most of these were sentenced to transportation for the crime of larceny, which carried a sentence of 7 years imprisonment or transportation at this time, though in one case, that of Margaret Gibbons, the sentence handed down

35 Ibid., July 13th, 1847.
36 Trevelyan, C.E. *The Irish Crisis*, p. 131.
37 Newman, Edward. Magazine of Natural History quoted in *The Way that I went*.

was 10 years transportation for sheep stealing. The Convict
Reference Book for the period reveals that only one woman
was transported in each years from 1845–1848. Generally,
sentences of transportation for larceny were commuted to terms
of imprisonment. Entry No. 12 in the Convict Reference Book
for 1849 tells us that those condemned for this crime had their
sentence commuted to an equal period of penal servitude.[38]

The case of Jane Bourke is interesting. She had been
sentenced to one year's imprisonment in 1845 for uttering
forged coin. She was sentenced to 7 years transportation for a
similar charge in 1848, but in her case as in others, her sentence
was commuted to 7 years penal servitude.

Men and women who were involved in the same crime and
were deemed equally guilty were treated in a different manner,
even though their sentences read the same. In 1848, May
Degnane was sentenced to 7 years transportation for sheep
stealing. Her sentence was commuted to imprisonment, while
Patrick Degnane who took part in the same crime and was
sentenced to the same period of transportation actually died on
Spike Island in 1851, while awaiting transportation. His sentence
had not been commuted. The Records show that almost all the
men sentenced to transportation prior to 1853 were actually
transported.

When sentences of transportation were commuted to
imprisonment, these were usually served in full unless prisoners
were released early from gaol, as might happen if there was an
epidemic in it. By 1853, the policy of transportation for relatively
minor offences was changed. Under the terms of the Penal
Servitude Act (1853), all crimes punishable by transportation for
less than 15 years were substituted by terms of imprisonment.
Thus, 4 years penal servitude replaced 7–10 years transportation;
6–8 years was the alternative to 10–15 years transportation. In
many cases, women who felt that they had been treated harshly
by the Courts appealed to the Lord Lieutenant to have their

---

[38] Report of Francis White, Inspector of Jails. *Mayo Constitution*,
November 25th, 1844.

sentences reduced, but the decision of this official was invariably unfavorable, although many sentences were harsh even by the standards of the time. A charge of larceny, which carried a penalty of 7 years transportation on conviction in 1847, was treated more leniently at a later date such as 1861, when ladies who had several previous convictions received sentences ranging from 2 to 4 years imprisonment with hard labor. Judith Carr who appeared at Swinford Court in 1861 was one of these.

Possible imprisonment, if convicted, did not prevent some women from committing crime. The court records for 1861 and 1862, for example, show that many women before the Courts in those years had begun, as teenagers, to steal during the Famine years. It would seem, that, having embarked on a life of petty crime, they felt they had little choice but to continue in that way of life. As theft was regarded as a social crime, a woman convicted of it would have found it almost impossible in normal circumstances to rehabilitate herself.

When one reads the list of convictions, one can conclude that the year 1860 seems to have been fairly prosperous in the County, as no woman was sentenced to penal servitude for larceny. This changed in 1861 and 1862, particularly in the Swinford area which had many convictions for this crime.

Some women may have become inured to a life in prison at this time and preferred prison life to that of begging or petty thieving outside prison walls. There is something very pathetic in reading about Bridget Dowd (nee McNulty) who was sentenced in 1862 to 3 years penal servitude for larceny. This lady was then aged 67 and one wonders how, at this age, she reacted to prison work and the harsh prison regime.

In the period under consideration, no woman in Mayo was sentenced to imprisonment or transportation for either vicious or serious crimes. The crimes which caused them to be sent to prison were caused by poverty and unemployment.

One can only admire the strength of character which motivated so many women to remain law abiding in one of the most difficult periods for them in the whole course of Irish history.

Education

In the sphere of education, women were victims of inequality and lack of opportunity. To place educational attainment in context, it is useful to look at the figures for Ireland in 1841, a few brief years after the National School system had been set up, while recognizing the contributions of other, sometimes older schools and teachers in this regard. Figures for illiteracy based on the 1841 Census are as follows:

Illiteracy by Age-Cohort and Sex (1841)

Age	16–25	26–35	46–55	66–75
	%	%	%	%
Ireland				
Males	34.6	38.5	43.1	45.8
Females	45.4	54.7	63.6	65.8
Total	**40.3**	**46.9**	**53.6**	**55.9**
Connacht				
Males	54.2	59.2	64.9	68.1
Females	70.2	79.2	85.1	88.1

Source: 1841 Census

While some progress in education was made in the decade from 1841–1851 (1851 Census), four out of every five women in the County were still unable to read or write in 1851.

% of Persons who could neither read nor write, who could read only and could read and white for the country as a whole in 1841 and 1851

Persons 5 years old and upwards who could read and write			
MALE		FEMALE	
1841	18%	1841	6%
1851	22%	1851	10%
Persons 5 years old and upwards who could read only			
1841	10%	1841	8%
1851	11%	1851	10%
Persons 5 years old and upwards who could neither read nor write			
1841	72%	1841	86%
1851	67%	1851	80%

Source: 1851 Census

There were several reasons for this. Besides the dearth of educational facilities in much of the County, girls then suffered from the widespread tendency of parents to give the best educational opportunities available to boys, which was particularly evident in poor rural areas. Girls in these areas suffered as a result. Girls living in or near towns generally received a better education. Educational provision was also very badly affected by the Famine in Baronies, such as Erris and Kilmaine which suffered the worst excesses of the Famine. They actually showed an increase in female illiteracy between 1841 and 1851.

To modern readers, it seems strange that progress had been made in getting learners to read or read and write, when increasing illiteracy was recorded in some Baronies. This suggests that girls who were enrolled attended schools for longer periods, until there were able to read at least, while an increasing number either did not attend school or attended for such minimal periods during this decade that they failed to acquire basic literacy skills.

Few men or women in the County as a whole could read in 1841. By 1851, there was an increase in the number of girls for the County as a whole who could read with a larger increase in the number of girls who could both read and write. This figure seems to suggest that more girls were attending school for longer periods than in earlier years. The progress made may mask the fact that more women than men were illiterate in the County throughout this entire period, particularly in remote poor rural areas such as Erris and Kilmaine, Baronies which also had the greatest number of male illiterates, revealing over-all educational deprivation.

Yet, despite the Famine, twice as many women in Erris were able to read in 1851 than in 1841, with a smaller increase in the number of women who could read recorded for Kilmaine, reflecting the greater efforts made to teach girls to read in these Baronies. The greater educational achievement recorded in 1841 was not sustained at this high rate over the next decade in some Baronies, Among them was Carra, with the lowest rate for female illiteracy in 1841, which showed a slight decrease in this figure in 1851 along with increased male illiteracy for the same period.

In Baronies, such as Murrisk, Burrishoole and Carra, reasonably well provided with schools, which had an increasing number of women able to read in 1851, there was also increased female illiteracy at this time. Famine and poverty were undoing the work of the schools at this time, when many girls did not attend school, or attended very poorly because of lack of food and clothing.

An analysis of education in the Barony of Tirawley reveals the true extent of illiteracy with more male than female readers in this period. In 1841, Rathlackan had the dubious distinction of having the highest percentages rates for illiteracy, followed closely by the neighboring parish of Lackan. By 1851, overall female illiteracy in Tirawley had fallen, though parishes, such as Lackan, still recorded very high rates. Two parishes, Kilfian and Rathreagh, bedevilled by poverty, the Famine, poor official

Relief works and reprehensible landlords recorded increases in female illiteracy. It is more difficult to account for the continuing high illiteracy rates in some poor parishes, such as Lackan and Rathlackan (7% increase in 1851); the local landlord, Sir Roger Palmer, as far back as 1821 had supported a free school for Catholics, with 18 girls on roll in that year.[1] The area was spared the worst excesses of the Famine; it had access to fish and other marine products supplies and had not sold off fishing equipment to procure food, unlike people in several coastal areas, forced to do so by poverty. It may be a question of values and it has been suggested that the fisherfolk of this area did not see much merit in education.

There were dramatic reductions in illiteracy in some rural areas, particularly near towns. Ballysakeery situated near the town of Ballina, which had a very high number of Church of Ireland and Presbyterian parishioners and excellent long established schools, is a case in point. However, conditions could vary considerably, even in neighboring towns, such as Ballycastle and Killala. There were more male than female readers in this Barony during the entire period. In 1841, a mere three women in rural Rathlackan could read. About one in seven women in towns such as Ballycastle and Ballina could read. By 1851, there were dramatic improvements in some nearby villages. Kilbride near Ballycastle and Templemurray not far from Crossmolina, showed an almost equal improvement.

Most women and men who could both read and write in 1841 lived in towns, with some boys outperforming the girls in literacy scores. In Crossmolina town, twice as many men as women could read and write. Parishes such as Kilfian had both a great increase in the number of women who could read and an increase in female illiteracy. Figures for districts such as Crossmolina in 1851 reveal that they had sustained their efforts to educate girls in the previous decade. Rural areas situated near towns stressed education to full literacy for girls. Proximity to schools and possible employment opportunities in neighboring towns may

---

[1]   Appendix No. 22. Education Ireland. P.P. Vol. XL, 1826, p. 1280.

have acted as powerful influences to ensure that girls received a basic minimum of education in such areas. The rural parish of Moygownagh recorded a great decline in female illiteracy. Older women in this parish, very many of them widows, recognized the need for education for girls. They certainly made great sacrifices to ensure some education for girls, helped by a free school in the parish.

The greatest numbers of women and a greater number of men, who could both read and write, were found in towns, such as Killala and Ballycastle. In Crossmolina town, twice as many men as women could read and write. The differences were not so great in Killala and Ballycastle. In rural areas, the situation for women was worse. In Addergoole, Kilbelfad, Kilbride, Kilfian and Moygownagh, male readers outnumbered female readers by about 5 to 1. Moygownagh made great efforts to educate both boys and girls. It showed a great increase in the number of girls who could read only, while four times as many males as females could both read and write in this parish. The many widows in this parish saw education as the key to upward social mobility for both boys and girls.

Of particular interest is the number of people who were in Public Institutions in this Barony in 1851, when women outnumbered men by 9 to 5. Of the 963 women inmates, one in 7 could read only, another 1 in 7 could both read and write and 832 could neither read nor write. One wonders how far their lack of education caused these inmates to be in these institutions. Those completely illiterate were more helpless in the struggle for survival than those who had received even minimal education. When a certain measure of literacy could mean obtaining some small position, or help if one emigrated, lack of education contributed greatly to women's difficulties.

By 1851, the overall number of men and women who could both read and write in the County had improved and continued to improve rapidly, particularly after 1860.

Why were the greatest numbers of women who could both read and write to be found in towns? An explanation may be the greater number of schools available, ease of access to these schools (a veritable barrier to children in remote rural areas), greater employment opportunities for those who were literate and parents' awareness of the advantages of education of girls until they were literate, reflected in better job opportunities and perhaps in the marriage stakes.

Of great interest also is the question of bilingualism. Even though instruction in Hedge Schools was carried out through English in this period, one is amazed at the spread of bilingualism, which was the norm rather than the exception. Baronies, such as Clanmorris and Carra, where English was in use before 1750, had a larger number of bilingual speakers than Irish speakers at all ages. In Clanmorris, bilingual speakers outnumbered Irish only by 2 to 1 and 3 to 1 in Carra. The Baronies where bilingualism was least evident at all ages were Kilmaine and Erris. Bilingualism was noteworthy in the age group 10–20 where bilingual speakers outnumbered Irish speakers by 5 to 1 for the County as a whole. Children in this age group may have begun to attend National Schools and learn English. Over the age of 90, there were more Irish speakers in 5 Baronies out of nine. This may not reflect the true position as so many people of this age had died.

Taking the County as a whole, the greatest number of bilingual speakers were under the age of 30. This spread of the knowledge of English seems to coincide in many cases with the advent of the National Schools, or where National Schools began to replace existing educational facilities, including Hedge Schools. Baronies, such as Murrisk, had a great variety of schools set up by several groups. These schools helped to teach English as far back as 1800, long before the coming of the National Schools. Migration, emigration and contact with the local gentry also helped to promote bilingualism. Seasonal workers in Scotland or emigrants in the U.S., who had a command of English, had an advantage over people unable to communicate in the language. Parents perhaps became more anxious that their children learn English once it was realized that a widespread flood of emigration had begun. For girls who stayed home, a knowledge of English was compulsory, if one wished to obtain any official position. After the Famine, the attraction of steady paid employment became more obvious to girls and more so to their parents, and so extra emphasis was placed on learning English so that a lucky girl might obtain a position receiving the 'Queen's pay'.

The age spread of bilingualism indicates that English was being learned on a fairly wide scale before 1770. In the year 1771, the Bishop of Killala noted that people who knew no other word of the language could curse in English.[2] It seems, however, that it was the National Schools which did most to promote the teaching of English in some Baronies after 1831. Erris and Kilmaine were the Baronies where the highest percentages of Irish speakers were concentrated and where bilingualism was least prevalent. These were the Baronies with the greatest problems of illiteracy and poverty. Bilingualism perhaps may also have been related to prosperity. Murrisk led the County in 1851 for First and Second Class Housing, while Erris and Kilmaine had the greatest number of Fourth Class Houses. About ninety-four out of every 100 people in Erris lived in either a Third or Fourth Class house.

Some interesting variations are clear when one looks at the statistics for the Baronies. Carra had five times as many bilingual as Irish only speakers for the age group 10–20. The average for the County as a whole was three times as many. This high figure may be explained not only by the coming of the National Schools, but also by the fact that many adult women in this Barony were bilingual and passed on their knowledge of the language to their children.

By contrast Erris and Kilmaine had a great number of bilingual speakers only between the ages of ten and twenty and had the greatest numbers of Irish speakers in the County. In Erris, in particular, the increased knowledge of English seems to be linked to the coming of the National Schools, as this was an area with a high rate of seasonal migration, and yet there was not a great number of bilingual speakers among the older age groups.

---

[2] *Archivium Hibernicum* (iii) (1914), p. 117.

Position of Irish only and Irish and English speakers in larger towns in County Mayo in 1851

Age Group	Westport		Castlebar		Ballinrobe		Ballina	
	Irish only	Irish & English	Irish only	Irish & English	Irish only	Irish & English	Irish only	Irish & English
0–10	–	7	3	49	11	4	2	60
10–20	6	86	8	431	23	27	2	287
20–30	10	140	7	178	13	19	1	196
30–40	7	177	4	155	18	12	3	161
40–50	7	122	9	155	14	9	14	147
50–60	7	123	6	104	9	7	9	104
60–70	7	78	6	79	5	6	12	14
70–80	2	22	2	17	1	1	8	17
80–90	2	9	3	12	-	1	2	7
90–100	4	-	-	3	-	-	1	1
Totals	52	762	48	1183	94	86	54	994

Source: 1851 Census.

The amazing growth of bilingualism over much of the County is the striking feature of this period. In much of the County bilingualism was the norm rather than the exception. In a Barony such as Tirawley, where one night have expected a very high percentage number of Irish only speakers, one is amazed at the number of people who were bilingual; there were almost four times as many bilingual speakers as Irish only speakers between the ages of 10–20. This was an area characterized by relatively good schooling facilities, a good proportion of towns relative to its size, a large rate of seasonal migration, and much emigration, particularly during the Famine and immediately afterwards from the ports of Killala or the more distant port of Sligo. Thus, many factors operated here to help the spread of bilingualism.

The spread of bilingualism in the towns of the County showed localized differences. All girls in Westport town under the age of ten were bilingual. Between the ages of ten and 90 many more women were bilingual. When one looks at the age group 30–40, one realizes how widespread the knowledge of English had become. One hundred and seventy seven women of this age could speak both Irish and English, while just 7 could speak Irish only.

Castlebar had a large number of female bilingual speakers. One third of the female population of 1231 were bilingual and a mere 48, or 1 in 25, spoke only Irish in this town. It could be argued that as a County seat, which also had a large garrison stationed within its confines, business in the town was conducted through English. This widespread knowledge of English was helped by the number of schools in the area, and opportunities for female employment in the town for those with a basic education, including English.

This pattern was not repeated in Ballinrobe where the female Irish only speakers out numbered bilingual speakers. There were more Irish only speakers over 30 in this town. In Ballina, as in Castlebar, there were more bilingual speakers up to the age of 90. In general, it was to be expected that bilingualism would be more widespread in towns than in rural areas, because of greater access to schools, volume of trade transacted, and employment opportunities for girls with a knowledge of English.

What kind of schools did girls attend? For many years, variety was the characteristic which most aptly describes the schools of the County, although many schools were becoming both democratic and standardized towards the end of the period with the spread of the National School system. There were many hedge schools in the County at the start of the period. Almost every sect had schools in the County in 1821, with the exception of the Society for the Discontinuance of Vice.[3] In this year the London Hibernian Society, which provided schooling for both boys and girls, had 41 schools in the County. The Baptist Church had 30. Among the Catholic population, there were 22 schools which were wholly or in part maintained by subscription, 227 pay schools but no Brotherhood of Christian Doctrine or Catholic Sisters.

---

[3]   P.P. Vol. LXV. 1821, pp. 348–350.

How many girls were enrolled in the schools which were provided? This is difficult to estimate, as few schools kept in a proper Register before 1831. However in the earlier years of this period, there was a higher male than female enrolment in schools. The picture within the parishes was very complex. In some parishes such as Islandeady and Achill, where there was no female teacher, female enrolment was very low. In Kilmore Erris, there were two free schools, one with 15 boys and 10 girls, and the second had 21 boys and 8 girls. A school for 19 Roman Catholics was maintained by subscription. In Killasser, the Baptist Society had three mixed schools, in each of which the boys outnumbered the girls who were enrolled, 184 boys and 130 girls. This pattern was repeated in the 2 Hibernian Schools in Swinford, which had 120 boys and 77 girls. Enrolment was more even in some of the schools in Kilmainmore, such as the Parochial School, which had 11 boys and 11 girls on the Register. This was also the case in the town of Westport where the Hibernian Society School had 45 boys and 45 girls. A few miles away in Aughagower there were 5 boys and 33 girls on the roll, which was exceptional at the time. In Moygownagh parish, 80 girls attended the free school in 1821. Ballysakeery had slightly more girls than boys in the schools set up by the Hibernian Society, the Baptist Society and the Trustees of Erasmus Smith. These figures could be very misleading, however, as in many instances, the boys were kept at home and the girls in this parish had a much higher figure for school attendance.[4]

By 1826, there were over twice as many boys as girls enrolled in the County schools.[5] Some areas in the County did much more than others for the education of girls at this time. In schools where there were no female staff, few girls attended. In Achill with 4 schools, there were no girls in two of them (Polranny and Achillbeg) and 5 in the other two. In the Castlebar area, far less emphasis was placed on the education of girls in Ballyheane than in nearby Turlough a few miles away. In Ballvoie, there were five

---

4   Appendix 5, P.P. XLV, 1826, p. 62.
5   Ibid., P.P. XLV, 1826, p. 32.

times as many boys as girls on the roll. This picture of a larger male enrolment continued, though not a necessarily larger male attendance.

In 1835, there was still great variety in the schools of the County. Ballinahaglish had 4 schools, including one Hedge School. Kilbelfad had four Hedge Schools. Kilcommin had 5 schools. There were more boys than girls enrolled in all the schools listed for these three parishes. The Parish of Doonfeeney showed one slight variation to the usual pattern of enrolment. There were 9 schools in this parish. In 8 of them, there were more boys than girls. The exception was a new school, founded a short time previously by Bridget Ormsby, which had 61 girls and 6 boys. The total for this parish was 349 males and 207 females on the school Rolls. Female enrolment was not as good in the Crossmolina area where 548 girls and 1140 boys were enrolled.[6] By 1842, when there were 69 national Schools in the County, 2,017 girls were enrolled in these schools and 4,467 boys.[7]

By 1851, 7,693 girls were enrolled in the schools of the County. This represented a great increase since 1841, when 3,675 girls attended school (national and other) in the whole County. Extra enrolment probably took place near the end of the decade, as the overall reduction in the number of women who could neither read nor write was a mere 6% between 1841 and 1851. It may also suggest that some girls at least spent little time in school and many who did may have left without becoming literate. The figure for literacy in the 1851 Census may not reflect the true picture as many literate girls may have emigrated during the famine years.

The variety in the types of school which girls attended began to disappear with the coming of the National Schools. Many girls were enrolled in the schools of Workhouses. In Westport Workhouse,[8] in 1851 there were 240 girls enrolled, of whom one was a Protestant. In this year, there were 324 boys and girls

---

6   Commission of Public Instruction, 1835, pp. 81d–87d.
7   9th R.N. Education, 1834–1842. Dublin 1844, p. 194.
8   Forbes, John, op. cit., p. 275.

in the school attached to Ballina Workhouse.[9] A high standard of excellence was maintained in these schools. The results may not have been solely due to the excellent teaching which these pupils received, but may also have been aided by better quality schoolrooms and better attendance at these schools, as well as the food which pupils in these Workhouses received, which was superior to that received by many poor pupils elsewhere. As evidence of the excellence achieved in these schools, Maria Fahy, a first-class teacher attached to the school of Swinford Workhouse received a premium for excellence. In the same year, 1851, Ellen Quigley, employed in the School attached to the Ballina Workhouse, received a similar premium. In general, only teachers who had passed through the Model Schools and were designated as being First Class were appointed to positions in Schools attached to Workhouses.[10]

Schools continued to be set up to fill local needs and very few schools were attended by pupils belonging to one religious persuasion. The Erasmus Smith Schools were attended by mainly Catholics and Protestant pupils, with a minority of Presbyterians.[11] The National Schools from which 'even the suspicion of proselytism' was banished, in the spirit of Stanley's letter, eased any fears parents might have about multi-denominational education. This worried Churchmen more than it did many parents, if one can judge by school enrolments.

Schools set up after the foundation of the National School system, but which did not belong to the system, showed a continuing trend of larger male enrolment. In such a school in Carrowmore in 1834,[12] there were 56 boys and 31 girls on the Roll, seven of whom were Protestants and 80 were Catholics.

There was a great effort to found National Schools in some areas despite the continuing opposition to them voiced by the then Archbishop of Tuam, John MacHale. In fact, the existence of free proselytizing schools may have acted as an incentive to

[9] Forbes, John, op. cit., p. 22.
[10] 18th R.N. Education 1851 – Volume II, p. 373.
[11] P.P. Vol. XL, 1826. Appendix No. 12, p. 156.
[12] O.S. Field Books (Mayo), p. 1067.

found National Schools in some areas. It must be emphasized, however, that many free schools did not function as proselytizing agencies. However, as the century progressed, a greater number of girls attended National Schools, which did much to make education democratic. Many girls who had begun to attend pay Schools were still on their Registers, when they became National Schools, which was most likely to happen, if the Pay School had been founded by a local Priest or landlord.[13]

Some areas became dotted with National Schools, organized by enterprising priests, such as Rev. Wm. Hughes of Burrishoole, who was responsible for eight Schools and the subsequent building of 5 replacement Schools.[14] By May 1840, there were 113 National Schools in the County. Seven of these were segregated, male and female. There were 3 female only schools in the County.[15]

Of particular interest were schools set up by various organizations to teach girls and boys skills as part of Famine Relief operations. Some were funded by the Society of Friends who saw education as the means of providing 'permanent relief' work. One such school was the Presbyterian School in Ballina.[16] These schools provided training in skills and also helped to relieve the poverty in pupils' homes. No bribes in the way of food or clothing were held out to Catholic children to attend it; but the girls received the profit on their own work and obtained all the materials at a cheaper rate. One can see why such a system was so much appreciated. The Belfast Ladies Industrial Association for Connaught aimed to 'qualify young females of Connaught to become independent members of society through their own industry.' They sent 54 teachers of approved qualifications to the West.[17] In the Westport area, 15 pupils in one of their schools had been beggars, two thirds of the girls in another school were orphans. Many educators felt that ongoing

---

[13]   Daly, Mary, op. cit., p. 159.
[14]   Ibid., p. 156.
[15]   7th R.N. Education, 1840–1842.
[16]   Forbes, John, op. cit., p. 17.
[17]   Society of Friends: *Transactions*, p. 438.

training in skills was needed and thus the National School for Girls in Ballina was an Industrial as well as an ordinary national School.[18]

Attendance figures for the period were very low, with a few exceptions, such as Ballysakeery Hibernian Society School, where in 1821 there was almost full attendance for girls, with an average attendance of 58% for boys. Sometimes boys were kept at home to work on holdings in Spring and Autumn, while girls were kept at school. The pattern of greater female than male attendance was also evident in Turlough Free School run by the London Hibernian Society. Some schools had very poor attendance records, such as Kilmurray Baptist School and the school at Nappagh in Aughavale, where an average attendance for both boys and girls was a mere 36%.[19]

One is surprised to find poor attendance records in towns, where pupils lived in close proximity to schools. In the parish School attached to the Protestant Church in Ardnaree, in 1851 there were 58 boys were enrolled, average attendance 25 (43%). The average attendance for girls in this school was less than half. This was not merely a matter of money, as many enrolled pupils did not pay the required fee. Before the Famine, 130 boys attended this school as well as 110 girls. Low attendance figures were also evident in Castlebar. In Castlebar Protestant School, the average attendance for enrolled girls was slightly over half.[20] This low attendance may have been caused by the apathy and despair into which people had sunk after the Famine. Ironically, some of the best attended schools were those attached to the Public Institutions such as Workhouses.

Low attendance figures in many rural schools is understandable, particularly in bad weather, when children had to travel a distance to school. These conditions did not apply in the towns; the lack of food and clothing were the usual reasons mentioned for poor attendance, both in town and country. The 8 National

---

[18] Forbes, John, *Memorandums*, p. 16.
[19] P.P. Vol. XL, 1826. Appendix No. 12, p. 40.
[20] Forbes, John, op. cit., p. 278.

Schools[21] in Burrishoole Parish were poorly attended where of the 3,011 pupils on Roll, a mere 376 actually attended. The parish Priest stated that the reason for this was the 'want of sufficient clothing to cover their nakedness.' His evidence is supported by one parishioner, Nancy Moran,[22] who said: 'There is a free school near enough to us. I would be anxious to send my children to it; if they could read and write they might one day or other better their lot but I could not send them to a public school in nakedness'. When Forbes visited the National School run by the Sisters of Mercy in Ballina, he found that the attendance figures had dropped since the previous year and was told that the absences were caused inter alia by the harvest, and the unfavorable effects of the recent election for the Member of Parliament. Although pupils were sometimes kept at home in Spring and Autumn to help with crops or to help their parents earn their living such as Widow Kilboy, the basic reasons for non-attendance were lack of food and clothing, an ongoing problem. Shortly after their arrival in Foxford in 1891, the Sisters of Charity opened a School. They found that attendance was low. Once again, the Sisters found that this was mostly due to the lack of clothing and food.

In fact, some of the proselytizing agencies which had plenty of 'meal money' used the incentive of free food to get children to attend their schools, a practice condemned by many Protestant Church Clergy and some lay Protestants as well as by Catholic Priests.

I have chosen the year 1841 to look at the ages of people attending Primary School. In that year, 3,484 boys and 1,099 girls between the ages of 5–10 attended these schools. There was an emphasis on keeping girls in primary school until the age of 15 in that year while there was a decline in the number of girls who attended superior schools after the age of 10, with a greater decline in those who continued in those who continued in these schools after the age of 16.[23]

---

[21] Appendix A, p. 376.
[22] Appendix A. Evidence of Nancy Moran, p. 372.
[23] 7th R. N. Education 1840–1842.

What was the curriculum of the schools like? In all schools, reading, writing and arithmetic were basic. Reading and English spelling were the first task. Older children were taught writing and figures. They was a variety in some schools. Girls who attended schools run by male teachers did not receive instruction in Needlework, which was very important in schools run by female teachers. In Kilbelfad, in one of its 4 Hedge Schools, T. Naughton taught Bookkeeping and Mensuration as extra subjects to his boys and girls. Miss Fletcher taught Geography in the school at Kilmoremoy. Under the National Subject System, the curriculum and textbooks became standardized. English was the medium of instruction in all schools, including Hedge Schools. In some schools, such as the Church School in Ardnaree, a period of the school-time was devoted to industrial work.[24]

Some women had positions in education. Even in 1821, one can see that women, particularly Catholic women, had begun to carve careers for themselves in this field. Pay and conditions for teachers varied from place to place and frequently left much to be desired. Generally, women were paid less than men and the salaries varied according to the type of school, the number and proficiency of the pupils. In 1826, Rebecca Kyle earned £6 and Margaret Whyte £3. In Carra, Aglish, Alicia Keogh earned £12, while Maria KcKeon was paid according to the proficiency of the pupils.[25]

Salaries were almost the same between 1826 and 1835. Bridget Ormsby, who taught in Doonfeeney, received £12 per annum from the Baptist Society. Ann McDonough, who also taught in Doonfeeney, received from 1s. 3d. a quarter from 54 pupils whose average attendance was 40 pupils. In Crossmolina, Catherine Coleman enjoyed a prosperity unknown to many teachers, as she had a house provided for her residence valued at about £2. 10. 0 per annum provided for her by Major Jackson. Her salary consisted of £10 yearly from the Baptist Society and about £4 from the Irish Society.[26]

---

[24] Commission of Public Instruction 1835, pp. 81d–85d.
[25] P.P. Vol. XL, 1826. Appendix No. 22, pp. 1256–1280.
[26] Commission of Public Instruction 1835, p. 86d.

Teachers who worked in National Schools received a fixed portion of their incomes from the Board of Education according to the Grade of Teacher to which they belonged. The balance of their salaries was made up by local contribution. The security of being able to count on actually receiving this Government salary was very important to women, as local contributions were undependable in many instances. In 1838, Miss O'Connor, who taught in Kilmoremoy National School, with an enrolment of 117 girls, received £8. 13s. 0d. from the Board of Education and £11. 7s. 0d. from private subscription through the Parish Priest. Miss Fletcher, who taught in the Infant Division of the same School, was much better off with a yearly salary of £30.[27]

Salaries for teachers from the Board of Education were low, even in 1842 and when increases were granted in 1857. Teachers were divided into 3 main grades. A male teacher (1st Grade) was paid £35 p.a. in 1842 and £46 in 1857. A female teacher (1st Grade) was paid £24 in 1842 and £36 in 1857. To complicate matters, the First Grade was subdivided into Three Divisions, with salaries being reduced proportionally. Second Class teachers were subdivided into Two Divisions, as were teachers classified as Third Class. Teachers in the Second Division of Second Class and in the Third Class categories were very poorly paid, with a greater gap between them and those in the First Class Category in 1857 than had been the case in 1842.[28]

Mistresses who taught Needlework received £6. The great advantage of receiving the 'Queen's Pay' in the form of a salary lay, not in the buying power of the money so paid but in the security it represented and in the guarantee of regular payments, which allowed women a measure of control over their finances, allowing them to plan financial expenditure.

Children attending many of the schools were quite unable to pay the fee required, particularly during the years of the Famine. Even in 1851, this inability to pay was widespread and we learn that many children who attended the Protestant School

---

[27] 7th R. N. Education 1840–1842.
[28] Ibid., p. 217.

in Ardnaree were expected to pay one penny or two pence per week. Few, in fact, paid anything and it was only through the great generosity of the Rector that this school could he kept open.[29]

If there was a free school in an area, it was not unknown that some unscrupulous parents, while insisting on sending their children to pay school, did not pay the teachers and threatened to send their children to the free schools, when teachers looked for their fees. We learn that the master at Hollymount was forced to threaten legal measures to be paid and, when he did so, the parents threatened to send their children to the free school in Ballinrobe run by the Hibernian Bible Society.[30] This case has been recorded, but one can be sure that it was not an isolated incident and that many women teachers also suffered from bad debts.

Working conditions for the period in question varied considerably. Schools were sometimes held in private houses. In 1826, Johanna Kyte ran such a school at Kill Street (probably Church St.), in Ballina. Conditions in the schools founded by the Erasmus Smith Foundation were good. In 1826, the condition of their school in Ballina was excellent. It was a handsome commodious house; which cost £450, £300 of which had been allocated by the trustees of Erasmus Smith. Some schools which were built by subscription were also quite good as at Aglish near Castlebar which was 'a large commodious house built by Chapel connections'. The school founded by the Kildare Place Society at Aglish cost £220.[31] In 1826, it could be stated that better school buildings and better working conditions for teachers obtained where funding was supplied by organisations, such as the London Hibernian Society and the Kildare Place Society. These very good conditions co-existed with very poor conditions. In Ballycroy, the school was 'built with sods'. Sibby Conway taught in a similar edifice in the parish of Shianmore. In the Barony of Gallen, in Lismurran, Mary Fitzgerald

---

[29] Forbes, John, op. cit., p. 17.
[30] Daly, Mary, op. cit., p. 159.
[31] P.P. Vol. XL, 1826. Appendix No. 11, p. 132.

taught in a 'bam'. In Cong, the school operated by William Joyce and his wife Winifred was held in a 'common thatched cabin'.[32] Poor conditions prevailed in most schools, particularly in the Hedge Schools, during the period. Even the coming of the National Schools did not represent an improvement in the working conditions for many teachers. Fr. Hughes, a very enlightened cleric, who did trojan work for education, built 8 National Schools in the Parish of Burrishoole. These were thatched cabins, each 14' x 12'. Later he replaced 5 of these. In the poverty of the time, these represented a substantial capital investment.[33] The National School at Cushen was a 'poor quality cabin 18' x 11', because the parish could not raise the resources to get a building grant. Overcrowding tormented teachers and pupils in schools then as now. The school at Newport was so seriously overcrowded that the overflow students had to be accommodated in the Chapel, contrary to the Commissioners' Rules.[34] By a strange turn of Fate, the best classrooms were probably to be found in the Schools attached to Workhouses and Gaols. When the Religious orders became involved in the teaching of girls, they built good schools and kept a high standard of hygiene in them.

Aside from cold, damp, overcrowded working conditions in many schools, one of the greatest deprivations suffered by teachers was a lack of teachers' residences. An Inspector of the Board of Education wrote that a teacher might have to walk many miles to and from his/her school and teachers on miserable salaries were often obliged to lodge 'in small houses or the confined dwellings of farmers who, for a sum of £1 or £1. 10s. per quarter, will 'oblige the Manager' by consenting to receive the teacher as a lodger on condition (most generally) that the guest occupy the kitchen during the evening, and at night retire to rest in a bed-room already shared by two or more members of his family.'[35]

---

[32]   P.P. Vol. XL, 1826, pp. 1264–1270.
[33]   Daly, Mary, op. cit., pp. 156–159.
[34]   Ibid., p. 160.
[35]   R.N. Education, 1863. p. 250.

Many teachers lived lives of quiet desperation. It was not until the work of Vere Foster began to take effect after the period in question that leaking roofs in many schools were repaired, wooden floors installed instead of clay ones, windows made open instead of being fixtures and proper privies were supplied. Even in 1858, an Inspector bemoaned that 2% of the schools were still wretched hovels – structures under the roof of which it is lamentable to have to gather together as many children as constitute a school, the means of ventilation are so bad, the lighting so imperfect, and the earthen floors so damp and unhealthy.

Generally, single ladies taught. In 1826, only one widow Mrs. Hall is listed as being a teacher. There were six married women teachers working in this year. Some parishes, such as Costello, had no lady teachers until the coming of the National Schools. Louisburgh had 16 male teachers and no female in 1826. Despite poor salaries and working conditions in Education, there were 43 women teachers in the County in 1826 and 167 by 1851. In 1826, there had been 311 male teachers in the County but this number had not greatly increased by 1851.[36] Women were slow to be appointed to some National Schools, and by September 1842, there were just 11 lady teachers in these schools and 63 men.[37] Many of these were single women and, as such, held a lower position in the community than the Master. It may be assumed that lady teachers in the County as elsewhere deplored not only the lower pay which they received but also about their very poor working conditions and consequently they were in the vanguard in the fight for women's rights by becoming Trade Union members, and thus the Irish National Teachers Organisation (I.N.T.O.) has consistently had more female than male membership.

While educational facilities had been improving during the period, the whole infrastructure of society meant that many pupils, both boys and girls, were unable either to avail of the

[36] R.N. Education, 1858, p. 182.
[37] 7th R.N. Education, 1840–1842.

opportunities provided, or to make best use of them. Poor housing, poor health, unemployment, bad food and clothing meant erratic attendance at school, as well as listless attention when present. This was particularly the case during the years of the Great Famine and during other lesser famines. Dread of fever also caused many children to be kept from school. Bad eyesight, caused by ophthalmia, which was endemic during the Famine, caused many children to lose at least one eye, causing extra hardship in attempting to deal with schoolwork, a difficulty aggravated by the dark conditions in the cabins when trying to do homework. Much more progress began to be made with the gradual improvement in public health, brought about to a great extent by the setting-up of dispensaries throughout the County and with the spread of the idea of positive health by attention to better food and cleanliness.

While formal education meant a great deal to women by removing the stigma of illiteracy, thus enabling them to take a more effective role in society and making them eligible for the few positions in employment that were available to them, one must not underestimate the great role which informal education played in the lives of women. Training schemes were set up under the heading of Famine Relief and administered by ladies of all religious denominations, as well as by female members of religious orders. Enlightened ladies, such as Mrs. Fannie Knox and the Belfast Ladies, saw the importance of teaching girls skills, thus making them employable and providing 'permanent relief'. They understood the multiplier effect of providing women and girls with education and training. When women were employed, there was a noticeable improvement in food and clothing provided thus enabling families to make better use of available educational opportunities. Schools, such as the excellent Presbyterian School in Ballina, not only taught girls skills, they also helped to relieve the poverty of their families at the same time, by the system which they operated. Later, the Sisters of Mercy by promoting the work of temperance and by teaching home management and thrift to the poor, helped not only to improve the quality of life and health of these poor people but also ensured that the effects of formal schooling were maximized.

Poor home backgrounds, food and clothing continued to affect the lives and education in poorer areas of the County, such as Foxford, where they were tackled by the Sisters of Charity. They improved public health by effecting the removal of manure pits from the thresholds of cabins, which helped to stop the spread of fevers with their debilitating effects. They began to promote positive health by training women and girls in the techniques of cultivating a kitchen garden. This was not achieved without opposition, as we read that the cultivators at one time refused to eat carrots as they were red and red vegetables could not be good! They continued the work begun by the Society of Friends of distributing seeds, thus helping the cause of nutrition and by spreading the 'gospel of cleanliness and thrift' effected a great improvement in health and an improvement in education standards.[38] The effects of the teaching and training in housekeeping and crafts carried out by all these good ladies helped dispel the slovenliness and squalor which were the characteristic traits of parts of the county. While dispensaries helped to lessen the spread of diseases, the work done in education spread positive health, thus helping to promote a better quality of life despite the widespread poverty while ensuring better use of the schools.

There was a great desire to have girls educated.[39] Mary Rich was a widow with three children who survived by begging all year round in Cong. She had moved there so that her children could attend the free school. She was one of many who made great efforts to get schooling for their children. With the coming of the National Schools, schooling became more democratic in principle. It is sad to think, however, that economic and social factors did not allow many children to participate fully in the national school system, particularly in its early years. By

---

[38] Finlay, T.A. (S.J.) Foxford, 'A Substitute for Socialism', New Ireland Review, Vol. XIV, September 1900, pp. 6–14.

[39] Appendix A. Evidence of Mary Rich, p. 500.

1851, some slight improvement had been made in the sphere of education although it was 1861, before the impact of the National Schools really began to be felt in the fight against illiteracy. Education was becoming more accessible and thus more girls could avail of it.

To obtain a position as a teacher was the ambition of many girls in the County, as it was one of the few official positions open to them. The salaries though low, were attractive, and gave women a certain measure of independence in their lives. Several girls who had received some education now began to apply for the post of governess and fourteen of them were so employed in the County in 1851.

More lady teachers seem to have been employed in teaching basic subjects in this period. The trend which later developed of having many lady teachers involved in the teaching of Music and Dancing had not begun by 1851. At that time, men taught dancing. There was just one lady teacher of Music in the County in 1851. Matters improved when the County became more prosperous and there were further opportunities for women as teachers of accomplishments.

13

1851 and After

The challenges facing women in Mayo in the years after 1851
were daunting. Ireland was a sick society, its social body ravaged
by the diseases of materialism and conservatism.[1] Women in
Mayo, as elsewhere, contended to the best of their abilities
with these stultifying forces. Conditions were still grim in 1850
when *The Nation* on 5 January 1850 stated: 'The high tide of
pauperism swells around the narrowing basis of social Ireland as
the Rhine flood rose against the dykes of Holland. Galway and
Mayo are sinking into swamps more fathomless than the Adriatic
marshes'. This quotation highlights the difficulties women faced
in the daunting task of rebuilding their lives from 1851 onwards,
a challenge made more onerous because of their position in
society, getting worse since 1800. Prevailing societal attitudes
are clearly reflected in some official documents. For example, the
1871 Census was the last to give a complete picture of women
in agriculture. Their skills were disrespected and downgraded in
the 1881 Census, as the wives, sisters and daughters of farmers
were now classified as 'persons not following any specified
occupation'. This occurred at a time, when developments
which might have been expected to assist them in the quest for
a better life, actually worked against women. The introduction
of technology into agriculture led to the commonly held belief
that women would not be able to deal with it, a belief which led

---

[1]   Lee, Joseph J. 'Women and the Church since the Famine'. In *Women
in Irish Society, The Historical Dimension*, eds. Margaret MacCurtain and
Donncha Ó Corráin, p. 42.

to the displacement of many women in agriculture,[2] on which so many of them depended for income.

Against this backdrop, women attempted the painfully slow work of regaining lost ground and carving a new niche for themselves in society. Women, who had endured the worst ravages of the Famine, were particularly concerned with gaining a measure of economic security, thus ensuring that neither they nor their families would ever again go hungry. This desire for security was more acute in rural areas, where few women had managed to retain a hold on their land.

The pattern of social life changed. Many girls, if unmarried, were no longer willing to remain at home, economically dependent, deferring to the authority of the woman of the house, be it mother, married sister or married sister-in-law. Marriage, which conferred status on girls, now took place at much older ages than had been common before the Famine. In many cases, the possibility of marriage in this country was ruled out, when a girl had no dowry. Emigration became more important. The Famine had overcome the traditional aversion to the emigration of girls, especially as there was a cumulative restlessness in those accustomed to migration from childhood.[3] However, attitudes towards emigration in general changed during the Famine years from 'panic-driven expulsion to a calculated pursuit of economic betterment'.[4] While it had positive effects on the lives of many women, there are mixed views as to the effects of emigration on Irish society. 'Emigration was an important strategy for survival for those who had the energy or the means to leave the country';[5] in fact, many prospered in the USA, for example, if they had the essential qualities of youth, soberness and a capacity for hard work.[6]

---

2   Luddy, Maria: 'Women and Work in the 19th and in the early 20th – An Overview' in *Women and Paid Work, 1500–1930* by Bernadette Whelan.

3   Fitzpatrick, David, *Emigration 1801–70*, p. 563.

4   Miller, Kerby A., *Exiles and Emigration*, p. 44.

5   Kinealy, C., *Death Dealing Famine* p. 118.

6   Schrier, A. *Ireland and the American Emigration, 1850–1870*, p. 27.

Taking the particular circumstances of their lives into account, many girls from Mayo, haunted by famine and unemployment, decided to emigrate rather than migrate, especially after the Famine. They were better fitted to seek economic betterment than girls of an earlier generation, as more of them were now literate. They generally settled in the industrial cities of England, and on the East Coast of the USA. Many became maids in the houses of the rich and some were later promoted to the post of housekeeper. (Several valued the accommodation attached to these posts). In many instances, these women did not wish to compete with migrant men for jobs in factories, especially textile factories, as they had grim memories of the decline of the textile industries in Ireland and feared a possible similar occurrence in the New World). Several remained single and if/when they married, they were often advanced in years. Many made great economic contributions to the welfare of poorer relatives in Ireland. In a way, American money was a tax levied on the filial piety of child emigrants.[7] While some would have been very proud of the improvements to housing, training for other family members, better standard of living, etc., effected by these remittances, as John Healy[8] describes his aunts and female relatives in *Nineteen Acres*, there can be little doubt that some girls resented both the fact that they felt compelled to emigrate by conditions at home and the expectations that they would continue to remit cash to distant relatives. That remittances represented considerable personal sacrifices is seen in the fact that most remittances from the USA came from a group 'composed largely of laborers and domestic servants'.[9] Several historians have bemoaned the undesirable effects of emigration on Irish society, leading to a culture of dependency. Oldham, for example, suggests that emigration contributed to the 'perpetual survival of the unfittest and the debasement of the

---

[7] Ibid., p. 113.
[8] Healy, John. *Nineteen Acres*.
[9] Schrier, op. cit., p. 110.

human currency in Ireland.[10] In time, some emigrants came to resent a fairly common attitude, which insisted on seeing them almost as victims.[11] 'Seeing them as exiles is condescending to the emigrants. It is unconsciously demeaning to the various new lands in which they settled for it treats the New Worlds as a set of Elbas where no one would settle by choice'. It was widely held, in a culture of limitation, that Irish girls had three choices, emigrate, remain single or be a nun. John Healy in *The Death of an Irish Town*, (Charlestown, County Mayo) repudiated this attitude. He argued that 'Each man has his own story and each girl her own reason for emigrating'.[12]

These migrant women also made worthwhile contributions to their adopted countries, helping to finance the building of schools and churches and supporting their countrymen and women during periods of unemployment. This use of personal funds to support family members, unemployed people, social projects in both Ireland and overseas led Tom Hayden in *Irish Hunger* (p. 15) to conclude that many girls emigrated 'in search of an American future that turned out to have a lot in common with the Irish past'.

There were great changes in the lifestyles of some women who remained at home. More of them were literate. As the reading of newspapers became more common, they were better acquainted with world affairs and new ideas. Most women who remained in the country still had to cope with apathy, poverty and unemployment; those in employment often worked in very poor conditions. It is significant that the more educated of these women, the teachers, who felt strongly about women's rights and social conditions, took an active part in the I.N.T.O. (Irish National Teachers Organisation) from its inception. They understood the force of the Union to effect change, and consequently, they outnumbered the number of men in the organization. What is interesting is the 'fact that (there was)

---

[10] Oldham, C.H., 'The Incidence of Emigration on Town and Country Life in Ireland' in *JGSGI*, Vol. xii, 1914, p. 231.

[11] Akenson, *The Irish Diaspora* (1996) p. 11.

[12] Healy, John, *The Death of an Irish Town*.

no large-scale, significant organization by women on their own behalf in Ireland from 1850 to 1900, corresponding to contemporary movements in Western countries'.[13] Unskilled female domestic servants often lived lives marked by deprivation. No regulations protected them and many were exploited shamelessly, because no other employment was available to them as so many girls were looking for posts as domestic servants. While domestic servants had a very low status in society, this does not appear to have troubled these girls very much. The struggle to survive was so grim that many women inured themselves to endure appalling conditions to earn a living. It was said that 'in Ireland the female worker has hitherto (1911) exhibited in her martyrdom an almost damnable patience.'[14] Indeed, it was not until 1911 that the I.C.T.U. formed the Irish Women's Workers Union to improve the wages and conditions of the women workers of Ireland. This did little to better the lot of girls in domestic service, as such workers are notoriously difficult to organize. Those girls employed in places, such as the Woolen Mills of Foxford, could count themselves extremely fortunate.

Women's changing role in agriculture is of interest as machinery dispensed with much physical labor supplied by females in earlier times. Few widows had retained a grip on their holdings,[15] sometimes with great difficulty. Most who did held land in joint leases, which caused perpetual acrimony. Many, however, leased their cabins in their own name. Several women rented small gardens and attempted to eke out a living from the produce of these gardens.[16] Conditions had not changed greatly for farmers' wives and they still continued to do all kinds of duties on their farms (as well as their domestic chores) until the end of the century.[17] 'The excessive struggle for

---

[13] Clear, C., *Social Change and Everyday Life in Ireland, 1850–1922*, p. 4.
[14] Connolly, James, cited in 'Women, the Vote and Revolution' in *Irish Society, The Historical Dimension*, p. 4.
[15] Griffith's Valuation.
[16] Ibid.
[17] Luddy, op. cit.

existence in the more remote agricultural districts' as recorded in The Special Inquiry as to Agricultural Holdings (1881) was a grim reality for many. Women played a large part in the Land Movement in the County, usually by supporting their menfolk in the organization. They also took an active part in the Ladies' Land League, during the Land War 1879–82. In fact, Anne Deane, from Ballaghadereen, then in Mayo, but later in Co. Roscommon, when County Boundaries were reorganized) was the first President of the League for a time. Beatrice Walshe of Balla was also to play a prominent role.[18] Rural women qualified for membership of the Land League, if they were tenant farmers in possession of the family farm. However, most female tenant farmers were widows. They jealously guarded this right in order 'to protect and preserve their economic interests', in the words of TeBrake.[19] In a society where they had little influence and few opportunities for making decisions which affected their lives, women realized how important it was for them to protect their homes, both for economic and personal reasons, particularly with the encroachment of technology into traditional working patterns, although in time several women decided to maximize their 'possible economic contribution (to their households) by focusing their energies into unwaged domestic work in an age when 'economic growth changed the material and labor requirements of the home[20] Women also took an active part in fund-raising for the League. The predominantly male League recognized that without the ladies' support, for instance, it would have been impossible to carry out the campaign of Boycotting, as they purchased goods for the household. Their labor helped greatly to effect Land Purchase as their earnings and thrift helped procure the money to pay the annuities. The cause of land purchase was especially dear to women who had

[18]   Meehan, Rosa, *The Story of Mayo* (2003).
[19]   TeBrake, Janet, 'Irish Peasant Women in Revolt: The Land League Years' in I.H.S. Vol. xxviii, No. 109, May 1992.
[20]   Bourke, Joanna, 'The Best of All Home Rulers', The Economic Power of Women in Ireland, 1880–1914, Ir. Econ. Soc. Hist, XVIII (1991), pp. 34–47.

endured rack rents, evictions and the torture of joint leases and helped to foster their sense of a better life. They still had to cope with high rents, emigration and partial Famines. The fear of hunger continued to haunt people who had experienced food shortages, even when they were emigrants. Emigration, however, was sometimes linked to improved living conditions, as cited in Miller (1985):[21] 'I can sit at a table as good as the best man in Belmullet ... thank God I left that miserable place'. The decade from 1870–1880 was marked by the collapse of the kelp industry, coinciding with the renewed appearance of the potato blight and adverse weather conditions.[22] In fact, the Congested Districts Board was set up to deal with the problem of poverty in the West of Ireland. A Congested District was one in which the ratable valuation divided by the number of inhabitants was less than thirty shillings.[23] Inspectors' Reports reveal a hard core of poverty which seemed impossible to eradicate which is reflected in house occupancy and in the numbers of Workhouse residents. A large amount of 4th Class Housing was still in use in 1889, with a strong link between poor buildings and poor holdings. This deprivation is also reflected in Workhouse figures. The Census of 1891 (Table 99/407) shows that up to 1885, the percentage of able-bodied women to the total Workhouse population, in both Mayo and Galway, was never less than eleven points higher than that of able-bodied men. Some of this could be accounted for by female unemployment and incapacity. For instance, there was also a higher percentage of women than men in the blind asylums attached to the Poor Law Institutions.[24]

One feels that in the field of politics, women in Mayo were more concerned with the politics of the Land Question which affected them immediately than they were with Home Rule,

---

[21] Miller, Kerby A., op. cit., p. 507.
[22] King, Carla, 'Our Destitute Countrymen on the West Coast: Relief and Development Strategies in the Congested Districts in the 1880s and 1890s' in eds. King and McNamara, *The West of Ireland, New Perspectives* (2011) p. 163.
[23] Moran Gerard, 'Near Famine: 'The Crisis in the West of Ireland 1879–1882' Irish Studies Review, v, No. 18 (Spring 1997) pp. 14–21.
[24] P.L. Reports, 1865–1892.

though the more thoughtful would have seen this as a long-term ambition.

Within the home, more literate women became receptive to new consumption patterns. They began to be influenced by the persuasive powers of advertising. The increase in money wages, as well as the development of the Parcel Post, enabled them to obtain articles not available to them previously and it became fashionable to procure items from shops, which formerly had been made at home. This change in consumption patterns which helped many women to set up small shops also marked the beginning of the decline in handcrafts. Managing consumption within households was critical to family welfare and survival.[25]

In the post-Famine decades, women in Mayo began to experience loneliness on a much larger scale than they had previously, as much emigration replaced migration. Young boys and girls who might have migrated to England and Scotland for the season, now began to emigrate to the USA or, on a lesser scale, to Australia and seldom returned to Ireland in the lifetime of their parents. Women missed the support and companionship of these children. The problem of loneliness became more acute for many women when a dispersed pattern of settlement became the norm and the older clachán settlements began to disappear. The physical conditions in which several women lived improved with the disappearance of much Fourth Class housing. Some legislation helped to improve both living conditions and housing, especially for the very poor. The Nuisance and Disease Prevention Acts, passed in 1848–9, governed the disposal of dirt and waste material. The Sanitary Act of 1866 did much to improve some people's lives as, under its terms, newly-appointed Sanitary Inspectors were charged 'with the maintenance of proper drainage, the supply of clean water to the populations of town and villages and the prevention of overcrowding in people's houses'. In rural areas, the Boards of Governors of the Poor Law functioned as housing authorities. They demolished many one-roomed cabins and did much to improve the living

---

[25] Luddy, op. cit.

accommodation of farm laborers from 1881–1886 by building laborers' cottages. The Laborers' Cottages and Allotment (Ireland) Act 'attempted to extend the provision of the 1881 Land Act to Laborers, which marked the first major housing enterprise in the British Isles'.[26] However, much drudgery still attached to housework in the absence of many household appliances.

There was a great rise in the scale of comfort in some cases. In 1878, however, Mayo was caught in the throes of the revolution of rising expectations and much distress present that year arose from the determination to maintain the comfort and rising standards visible in the County and not to resort to the old state of misery.[27] There is no doubt that women in the County were motivated in their actions by a grim determination both to prevent a return to the misery of their earlier lives and to have a better life for themselves and their families. While there was a vigorous leadership among the men of the County who wished to bring about great changes, it was the women of the County who made these changes a reality by their hard work, ability and determination. 'It had passed into an article of religion ... that the whole business of life was to succeed, no matter by what means'[28] in the words of Canon Sheehan.

The education many women received contributed greatly to the 'rising expectations' which were apparent in Mayo from 1860 on. Mayo women realized the importance of formal education as the means of upward mobility, independent income and a certain status in society, which was not always forthcoming.

Census figures for 1841–1871 reveal an amazing growth in literacy and a decline in illiteracy from 53% to 33% for the country as a whole during that period. This decline is all the more remarkable taking into account the disaster of the Great Famine, other near famines, political unrest and the poverty

---

[26] Aalen, Frederick, 'The rehousing of Rural Labourers under the Laborer (Ireland) Acts, 1883–1919' in The Journal of Historical Geography, Vol. 12. Issue 2, 3July 1886, pp. 287–301.

[27] Lee, J.J., *The Modernisation of Irish Society*.

[28] Sheehan, Canon, *The Blindness of Dr. Gray*, (1909), p. 224.

of the time. There is little doubt, however, that some literate women in paid employment felt a sense of frustration; they might reasonably have expected an improvement in their status in the community because of their earning capacity. However, this did not happen in many instances, as women's wages were absorbed into the household budget.[29] It was also felt that women's work within the family was part of the informal economy and, as such, received little recognition.

In spite of this prevailing attitude, however, it is certain that strong, independent minded women did not allow themselves to be defined by it. They recognized the intrinsic work of their work within the family, 'when managing consumption could (and did) make the difference between subsistence and going to the Workhouse for poorer families.'[30]

Because so many women in the County received little formal education, particularly in the earlier years of the period under discussion, it would be erroneous to conclude that they were therefore uncultured. Women of the County, whether literate or not, were heirs to the wealth of Irish tradition with its folklore, sagas and native music and poetry.

In this work, I attempted to delineate the 'realm of women (in Mayo, at a turbulent period in the history of the country) whose existence lay 'hidden below the master narratives of male history',[31] a labor of love.

Sin a bhfuil.

---

29 Luddy, Women and Work pp. 44–57.
30 Ibid.
31 Brink, André, *Imaginings of Sand* (1996).

Addenda

THE CONACRE SYSTEM

The term conacre appears to mean a contract by which the use of a small portion of land is sold for one or more crops, but without creating the relation of landlord and tenant between the vendor and vendee, it being rather a licence to occupy than a demise. The term is likewise and perhaps more correctly applied to the land held under such a contract ...

In Connacht, conacre was frequently taken for the purpose of raising crops of oats, hay and flax as well as potatoes, though mainly for potatoes.

The Digest of the Devon Commission defines conacre clearly, as follows:

> Generally, the vendor manured the ground and performed all the labor required to prepare for the reception of the crops. It enabled may farmers without capital to pay their rents. The price for conacre land, however, was very high, frequently pushed up by middleman.
>
> The evil of the system was that the hirer was exposed to the full risk of the year's crop being bad.

James Caird condemned the system in graphic terms in 1850:

> Nothing has contributed so much to the entire dependence on the potato and the consequent increase of a miserable, half-fed naked population, as the system of Conacre labor. This system is fatally interwoven with the social conditions of the West of Ireland.

Caird also argued for a total change in the agricultural management of the country as being the only remedy for the dire straits in which it found itself.

James Caird: *The Plantation Scheme in the West of Ireland as a Field for Improvement.* London (1850)

COTTIERS

Cottiers, who were virtually landless laborers, were closely linked to the conacre system, which was strongly denounced by James Caird. Winstanley (2007) has calculated that there were 596,000 of them in Ireland in 1841 and were the largest single occupational group then in the country. While it is sometimes thought that the peasant population was homogenous, the situation in rural areas was far more complicated. Cottiers, in fact, occupied the lowest rung of the social ladder.

With the decline in prices for agricultural produce after 1815, the decline in cottage industry, coupled with fewer opportunities for seasonal employment and high rents, which they had to pay for the use of land (generally of the poorest quality) to which they had no leases caused many of them to live at subsistence level, with an over-reliance on the potato for food, the cottiers as a class had virtually disappeared after the Great Famine. The demand for conacre caused by the competition for land and labor enabled those letting land on that system to demand and receive high rents, which were unsustainable in the long run.

WHERE THE CROY POURS HER CLEAR WATER INTO CLEW BAY

Among the hills of old Mayo
My parents had their home
At Shean More where dawned
My natal day.

Ah weary years have passed since then.
In foreign lands I roam,
And now I'm drawing near
Life's closing day,
I'd like to visit Erin's Isle
And see the ocean's foam
Around the storm swept shores
Of old Clew Bay.

My dearest earthly wish would be
To sleep in Erin's Isle,
And mingle with my sires
In death my clay
In the quiet ancient church yard
Of old Ballycroy,
Near the wind and wave washed waters
Of Clew Bay.

by Neill Joseph Caffrey*

This is a poignant poem of exile from the period, expressing the poet's love of his country, his memories of his native place, his wish to die in Ireland and be buried with his ancestors, (often expressed in Gaelic as a poet's wish for Bás in Éirinn), in beautiful Ballycroy, now a National Park.

* Neill Joseph Cafferkey was born in 1843 in Ballycroy. His father, Patrick Cafferkey, was born in 1812. His mother, Mary Conway, who was born in 1818, was a niece of Bishop Hugh Conway. Her grandmother, Mary Conway, (1768–1839) who is buried in Fahy graveyard was the mother of Fr Michael Conway and Bishop Hugh Conway.

I am indebted to Dr Sarah Pender, a descendant of Neill
Conway, of Placerville, CA for this poem. The Conway family
changed their name to McCaffrey in the New World. They
are a fine example of the wonderful contribution made by so
many people of Irish origin made, in their respective fields of
endeavor. to the countries in which they were settled, in this case
the USA.

EXTRACTS FROM DISTRESS PAPERS RELATING TO THE RELIEF OF DISTRESS AND STATE OF UNIONS IN IRELAND (FAMINE RELIEF PAPERS)

1. Evidence of Catherine Coyle, sworn in Irish by an interpreter:

'Am the widow of Anthony Coyle. My late husband was
for the last twenty years tenant to Mr. John Walsh, on the
townland of Mullaghroe. I was his second wife, and have
been two years married. My husband paid Mr. Walsh £3.0.0
a year rent. About the first of November, William Heffron
(who acts as agent of Mr. Walsh) accompanied by another
man, came to the house to demand possession of the house
and my husband gave it to them. He was re-admitted by
Heffron who gave him three or four weeks to prepare to
leave the house. Shortly before Christmas Day, William
Heffron and another man came into the house and told us
to leave – that he might throw it down. We all went out,
my husband and his four children and I am and the two
children he had by me quitted the house. The house was
thrown down the moment we quitted it. We returned to
the ruins and lived in a comer of it, having made a sort of
tent there. The tent was thrown down by Heffron shortly
after Christmas. I was not in at the time, but my husband
and children were. Since then we have been begging about,
sleeping wherever we could get lodging. About a fortnight
ago we came to the Workhouse. For six weeks before we

had been getting relief food from the Relieving Officer. My husband was in a dying state when he came to the Workhouse and has since died. He was a strong man when our house was thrown down upon us.

Sworn before me this 20th day of March 1848.
Richard Bourke, Poor Law Inspector.

2. Evidence of Catherine Hallon. She states: That being near her end in this world she has a disinclination to take an oath, never having taken one in her life, and not knowing the nature of an oath; but she declares what she is about to state to be the truth and nothing but the truth.

Being examined through a sworn interpreter, she states ... 'That she lived at Mullaghroe, on Mr. Walsh's property. She had a house and one and a half acre of land, for which she paid 30s. to Mr. Ruane, Fr. Walsh's agent. Owed a year's rent. Lived there all her life. Was never served a notice to quit, nor was her house, to her knowledge, taken possession of until about the month of September, when upon her return from the sea-shore one day she found the roof thrown in. She was told by the villagers that William Heffron, Mr. Walsh's steward had thrown the roof in, and that he had the sheriff's boy with him.

She made up a hut against the walls of the house and remained for about a fortnight in it, when one of her children having died she left the place and went out through the country to beg. Has been an inmate of the auxiliary workhouse at Binghamstown since the 9th of February.

Binghamstown 31st March, 1848.
(Signed) Pat Culkin, Sworn Interpreter,
Witnesses,
R. Hamilton, Temporary Law Inspector.
W.J. Hamilton, Temporary Poor Law Inspector,
John D. Waters, Vice Guardian

John Walsh (of Dublin) but married to a lady of the Cormack family of Castlehill was a Catholic. However, 'he was as hard on his tenants as the more extreme absentee landlords. He evicted tenants who failed to pay the rent and for any infractions'. Donohoe, (2003), pp. 249–250.

SELECTED DATA FROM THE REPORTS OF INSPECTORS OF THE CONGESTED DISTRICTS BOARD FOR IRELAND FOR SOME AREAS OF DISTRESSED UNIONS IN COUNTY MAYO, SUBMITTED IN DECEMBER 1892.

Distress was a notable feature of life in much of Mayo for many years after the period in question despite voluntary emigration, schemes of assisted emigration, improved education, the provision of houses for farm laborers, remittances from emigrants, the work of several charitable organizations and the work of the Congested Districts Boards. The Reports compiled by the Inspectors of the Board, some more detailed than others, provide interesting insights into rural life where much of the pattern of earlier rural life remained relatively unchanged, despite the upheavals of the century. Inspectors refer to the attempts of the population to be self-sufficient, even if they felt, on occasion, that their efforts were inefficient and some of those they were attempting to help were indolent.

Figures for both a better off family and a poorer family in the Beldergmore (a seaside area) are of interest as are those for the inland area of Pontoon, with its easy access to Lough Conn and Lough Cullen. Data relating to Beldergmore (p. 341) reveal that for a poorer family 'A bad potato crop would cause the great majority of the people to be 'brought face to face with utter destitution'. The Pontoon area seems to have been more prosperous; references to better doors and windows in houses in the Crimlin area would seem to suggest more disposable income.

In Achill Island, the income for a typical poor family was £17, £10 of which came from the proceeds of migratory labor and remittances from the U.S. What was surprising was the large expenditure on tobacco. Figures given, in some instances, do not include the value of products which were home produced, which were vital to the survival of families at subsistence level, such as the peat saved, essential for survival and kelp saved to provide fertilizer for poor land.

Women in these areas continued to earn cash, as they had during the Famine. In the district of Newport and Mulranny, income generated by the sale of eggs and poultry was very important. It was noted 'that thousands of eggs are annually sent to the English and Scotch markets from the district'. Similarly, in the Belderrigmore area of North Mayo, there was 'an enormous trade in eggs'.

The dietary in these areas had not changed much since the Great Famine. Maize continued to be used when potatoes became scarce. Although more cash was in circulation, a system of barter continued, particularly in relation to obtaining food. Many families were indebted to shopkeepers, some of whom charged high rates of interest (10%–15%) on outstanding balances, often cleared when migrants returned. Some of the barter may represent the activities of some cash-starved clients to obtain goods, without incurring further debt.

Eggs and corn were frequently exchanged for tea, sugar and tobacco.

With reference to clothing, the figures supplied for the Pontoon district point to the continuation of an earlier pattern, where men's expenditure on clothing was much greater than that for the girls and women, who may have attempted to redress the balance by using their skills in knitting, sewing and weaving to clothe themselves at minimum cost. There was a residual knowledge of weaving in some areas. Needlework formed an important part of the curriculum for girls in the National Schools and was valued by the girls themselves and their parents. Methods used to obtain clothes were often influenced by patterns of employment, emigration and migration. In Achill Island, 'clothes were principally bought in England and Scotland'. CDB Inspectors' Reports p. 341. Some migrants sent money home for the purchase of wool for the purpose of making flannel (much valued) and knitting socks. In some areas, such as Ballycastle, clothing was generally home-made, consisting of frieze and flannel, with cotton and calico being bought in Ballycastle or Belmullet.

The traditional gender divide with regard to the provision of footwear still applied. On the 19th December, 1892, the Inspector's Report for Ballycastle stated:

> 'Women wear no boots, except on Sundays or when they go to fairs or markets. On such occasions, they travel barefooted to and from town, merely wearing the boots during the time they remain in town'.

Many resident in the areas served by the CDB lived on small holdings in Fourth Class Housing. Most of these women were tenants at will or existed in sub-let holdings; some attempted to live off the produce of their gardens. However, it would be a mistake to conclude that many of them were down-trodden, as some exhibited a capacity for trade and the acquisition of property, often property to let, usually but not exclusively with a town address. Mary Boyd, in the parish of Aglish near Castlebar, let eighteen holdings, on which fourteen houses were built. In Belmullet, Margaret Davis, who was widowed, let eight houses. They are but isolated examples of the business acumen exhibited by some women in the County.

Inspectors of the Congested Districts Board were preoccupied with how to improve the standard of living for people living in their districts. The proposals contained plans for improved infrastructure, including the building of piers and the extension of the ill-fated branch line into Achill Island, upskilling in agriculture, training of girls in crafts, such as Lace-making in Lace Schools. There was a strong demand for Irish lace overseas for a number of years at this time, providing much needed cash for girls trained in these schools. A contemporary account reads as follows: 'One of my earliest memories is of the grown-up girls of my village (Ross) coming home from the Lace School (in Ballycastle) with their neat little baskets open, one could only wonder at the neat and tidy appearance of the contents'. (Unpublished Mss. Tom Langan, N.T.)

The seemingly slow progress to eliminate poverty in deprived areas in the County should be placed in the context of the time, in an era of slow communications and in the absence of infrastructure which would have greatly assisted those tasked with efforts both to relieve poverty and provide viable means of employment. In modern times, similar attempts in disaster areas have proved painfully slow in many instances. The fact that the problem of poverty seemed intractable in some parts of the County must be placed in juxtaposition with the huge improvements in other parts of the County. There may also have been a question of values. When was one well off? A telling comment was passed by the CDB Inspector, R. Ruttledge Fair (p. 315) on the Beldergmore Electoral Division:

'Families who, in this district, are considered fairly well off, would in almost any other part of Ireland be thought very poor', a reminder that prosperity and poverty are relative. By contrast with some years previously, people's economic situation had improved somewhat in this district, although most still lived at subsistence level. It is doubtful, however, if many in the area would agree with the comment published in *The Galway Vindicator* in January 1875 that 'Prosperity is the thing in the world we ought to trust the least'. For many, attempting to improve the lot of residents over several years, the comments of an active, faithful curate in Louisburgh struggling to mitigate the suffering of his parishioners during the Famine could equally apply to their efforts. To Asenath Nicholson, recorded in Annals of the Famine, he stated that 'his efforts were like throwing dust in the wind lost, lost forever – what is repaired today is broken down tomorrow'.

In modern times, despite the advances in education, modern technology, transport and communication, attempts to improve the lot of the disadvantaged in many parts of the world appear to progress very slowly. The efforts and achievements of earlier workers in the field are all the more commendable taking the circumstances of the time into consideration.

The indomitable spirit of the people in these areas, their resilience and their capacity to adapt to changing circumstances have proved potent factors in their survival.

Kilfian Parish Register from 1827 to 1836

This Register was kept by Fr. Michael Conway. A fire damaged later years of this Register, and further records for the Parish were not available until many years later.

MARRIAGES

11/2/1827   John Ormsby and Mary Langan
             Witnesses: John Deane and Hanna Langan.
             No Kindred.

20/2/1827   John Walsh and Sally Langan, Ballintober
             Witnesses: John Walsh and Mary McAndrew.
             No Kindred.

22/2/1827   Peter Lavelle and Sally Hardy, Balagone.
             Witnesses: Mary Flaherty and Elizabeth
             McLoughlin. No Kindred.

27/2/1827   William Reape and Hanna Langan, Ballybeg.
             Witnesses: Anthony Breen and Bridget Loughney.
             No Kindred.

17/3/1827   John McHale and Bridget O'Boyle, Belladoone.
             Witnesses: Henry McHale and Mary O'Boyle.
             No Kindred.

27/2/1827   Patrick Cavish and Cecily McKeon, Creevy.
             Witnesses: Patk. McAndrew and Bridget Lynott.
             No Kindred.

19/2/1828   Patrick Langan and Mary Divine, Bellagoan.
             Witnesses: Mick Kearney and Bridget Loughney.

24/11/1828   Thomas Roach and Winifred Reape, Kincon.
             Witnesses: James Langan and Winifred
             McGloughlin. No Kindred.

20/8/1829   Patk. Gordan and Anne Slack, Annaghmore.
Witnesses: Hugh McLoughlin and Anne Langan.
The woman a convert – first marriage in Church?

7/1/1830   Michael Langan and Catherine Ford, Kincon.
Witnesses: James Langan and Bridget Reap.

20/3/1830   Patrick Mullarkey and Catherine Langan, Tonroe.
Witnesses: James Healy and Jane Gardiner.

21/2/1830   John McDonnell and Honora Langan, Ballinkin-
littragh. Witnesses: Patrick Gaughran and Mary
Langan.

6/2/1831   John O'Neill and Mary Langan, Carrakeel.
Witnesses: Neale Conway and Biddy Nealin.

20/1/1832   Peter Collins and Mary Langan, Annaghmore.
Witnesses: Peter Cooper and Mary Cooper.

19/2/1833   Martin Healy and Mary Langan, Kincon.
Witnesses: Edmund Newcome and Catherine
Garvin.

25/3/1833   Thomas Langan and Anne Loftus, Ratheskin.
Witnesses: Martin McAndrew and Mary O'Hara.

Difficulties faced by emigrants in the United States

While many difficulties faced Irish families who were able to emigrate together to the USA, far greater vicissitudes faced those who went singly. Families were separated. Many lost contact with their families, whether through force of circumstances or by design.

I enclose a few advertisements which featured in The Boston Pilot, during this period. It was my great privilege to have been made aware of these advertisements during my visit to Boston a few years ago. In later years, papers published in other centers such as New York carried similar advertisements. One can only guess at the sorrow and heartbreak behind some of these advertisements and can only hope that at least some of them had a happy ending.

INFORMATION WANTED

1 August 1846. Of Thomas Barrett, formerly of Crossmolina, Co. Mayo who left Boston about three months ago, leaving a wife and five children in a state of destitution. It is supposed he has gone to Milwaukie, where a brother of his lives. Any information respecting him will be thankfully received by his wife.

17 April 1847. Of Mary and June O'Hara, natives of Co. Mayo, who left home in May 1846 and landed in Quebec. When last heard from they were in Henshenbrook, Lower Canada. Any information of them will be thankfully received by their brother Patrick O'Hara, now residing in Pottsville, Schuylkille County, Penn. Also, of his father and mother, John and Judy O'Hara, and

brother John O'Hara, who left Ireland in November 1846, and landed in New York.

27 November 1847 of Anthony and Patrick Water, natives of Co. Mayo. They are informed that their sister, Mary, who was married to Patrick Boyle, is anxious to hear from them. Her husband died on the passage. Write to her immediately, care of the Editor.

24 June 1848 of Sibby Flinn (her maiden name is Merrick), who sailed from Liverpool 25th June, in the ship *Julius Caesar*, landed in Quebec with 4 children – Mary, John, Bridget and Martin. Belongs to Ballina, Co. Mayo. She has not been heard from since. Any information from her will be thankfully received by her husband, Anthony Flinn, care of John Morrison, 86 Main St., Buffalo, N.Y.

(This family were still not fully united in 1850, as seen by the following notice).

26 January, 1850 of Debby Flynn, daughter to Anthony Flynn. She is a native of Ballina, Garden Street. She emigrated to America in 1847 and landed in Quebec. Her father is anxious to hear from her ... care of Patrick Crowley, Lackawana Iron Works, Luzerne County, Pa.

This story has a happy ending, however. In June 2001, Sibby's granddaughter, Kay Wilder of Florida informed the author that the family were reunited. Anthony had managed to buy a farm by 1851 and settled in Scranton, Pennsylvania, the current home of some family members. Anthony's persistence and his efforts over the years, not only to reunite his family, a Herculean task in the America of the time but also to get established in the New World, are truly admirable. He achieved all of this in a comparatively short period before his death.

27 January 1849 of Edmond McNulty, from Rathmacostello, Crossmolina, who came to America about two years ago and worked in Pennsylvania. He sent home £5.10. o. to his wife whose maiden name was Mary Hart from the parish of Moygownagh. He heard that she landed in the parish of New

York about 2 months ago. Any information will be thankfully received by his brother, John McNulty of Cabot ville, Ms.

11 May 1850 of Mrs. James Nugent (widow), native of Ballina, Co. Mayo. She sailed from Killala in the *Frances* Whitehaven 29th May last, bound for Quebec. There was a young man named Thomas Burns, printer and sister, with her. She was told to call at Mrs. Finigan's, Daltemaclas Street, Quebec. No account of her since. She is supposed to be with her son, Thomas Nugent, miller, between Upper and Lower Canada. Write to James McKeon, Cooper, 24 North Ferry Street, Albany, N.Y.

12 October 1850 James Barrett, of Mayo, Ireland, about ten years of age wants to find his sisters Mary or Biddy Barrett, who have been in Boston about three years. He is with James Corrigan from Donegal, aged about 12, who is looking for his father. Both of the boys were sent by some parties from Montreal to Boston. Both boys are entirely destitute. Information will be cheerfully received by J.B. Monroe, 59 Munroe, 59 Long Wharf, Boston.

Bibliography

ABBREVIATIONS

Appendix A with supplement
   Poor Inquiry Ireland: Volume XXXII, 1835.

Appendix D:
   H.C. Parliamentary Papers. Volume XXXI, 1836.

Appendix E with supplement
   Poor Inquiry (Ireland). H.C. Parliamentary papers, Volume XXXIII, 1836.

Devon Commission
   Digest of Evidence taken before Her Majesty's Commissioners of Inquiry into the State of the Law and Practice in Respect to the Occupation of Land in Ireland. Part I, Dublin 1847. Part II, London 1848.

Society of Friends: *Transactions*
   Transactions of the Central Relief Committee during the Famine in Ireland 1846–1852.

Forbes, John: *Memorandums:*
   Memorandums made in Ireland in the Autumn of 1852. 2 Vols. Land 1853.

Simms, W.O. *Narrative*
   Narrative of the 5th and 6th Weeks of William Forster's visit to some distressed districts in Ireland. Dublin 1847.

R.N. Education
   Report of the Board of National Education.

OFFICIAL SOURCES

Census 1821: P.P. Volume LXV, 1821.
Census 1841: British Parliamentary Papers, Vol. II, Session 1843.
Census 1851: British Parliamentary Papers, Vol. XIV, 1851.
Census 1911: Ireland.

CONDITION OF POOR

Poor Inquiry Ireland. Volume XXXII, 1835. British Parliamentary Papers, Volume XLV, 1835.
First Report from His Majesty's Commissioners for the Inquiry into the condition of the Poorer Classes in Ireland, 1835.
British Parliamentary Papers, H.C Vol. XXIV, 1836, Appendix G.
British Parliamentary Papers, H.C. Volume XXXI, 1836. Poor Inquiry Ireland. Volume XXXIII, 1836.
Distress Papers.
4th Series: Volume II.
5th Series: Volume II, 1847–1848.
6th Series:
7th and 8th Series: Volumes 4–8, 1847–1849.
Third Report Emigration 1827.
Royal Commission on Labour: Agricultural Labourers (Ireland) Volume XXXVII, 1893–1894.

EDUCATION

Reports of the Commission of Public Instruction. 1834–1835.
Reports of the Board of National Education, 1840–1842, 1851, 1858, 1863.

LAND

Devon Commission: Digest of Evidence taken before Her
majesty's Commissioners of Inquiry into the State of the Law
and Practice in respect of the Occupation of Land in Ireland,
Part I, Dublin 1847; Part II, London 1848.
Ordnance Survey Field Books (Mayo).
Griffith's Valuation: Mayo and Galway.

GENERAL INFORMATION

Thom's Directories.
Dublin Diocesan Archives 1829, 1849 (Archbishop Murray's
Correspondence).

CRIME

Transportation Registers 1845–1862.
Convict Reference Book 1845–1862.

JOURNALS

American Historical Review, 77 (1972).
Archivium Hibernicum (iii), 1914.
Béadoideas V and VIII.
Irish Ecclesiastical Record, Vol. LXIX, November 1947.
Irish Economic Social History, XVIII, (1991).
Irish Historical Studies, Vol. xxviii, No. 109, May 1992.
Irish Studies Review No. 18 (Spring 1997).
Journal of Social History (ix), 1975.
Studia Hibernica No. 13, 1973.
Studies IV.
New Ireland Review, 1900.
North Mayo Historical Journal.

PRIVATE CORRESPONDENCE

Sisters of Charity, Foxford.
Sisters of Mercy, Ballina.

NEWSPAPERS

Mayo Constitution
Tyrawley Herald
Saunder's Newsletters
Illustrated London News
The Nation
Galway Vindicator
Western People
The Sunday Times

BIBLIOGRAPHY OF PRINTED SOURCES

Aalen, Frederick H.A., 'The rehousing of Rural Labourers under the Labourer (Ireland) Acts, 1883–1919' in Journal of Historical Geography, Vol. 12, Issue 2, 3 July 1986.

Akenson, Donald H., *The Irish Diaspora: A Primer* (Toronto, 1996).

Armstrong, Frank, 'Blight of boom and bust is of our own making', in *The Sunday Times*, 4th January, 2015.

Bowen, D., *Souperism, Myth or Reality: A Study of Catholics and Protestants during the Great Famine* (Cork, 1970).

Beaumont, de G., *L'Irlande*, Brussels (1839) translated by David Thomson Blackstone (London, 1936).

Brink, André, *Imaginings of Sand* (New York, 1996).

Caird, James, *The Plantation Scheme or the West of Ireland as a Field for Improvement* (London, 1850).

Campbell, Ake, 'Irish Fields and Houses' in Béaloideas V, No. I, 1935.

Corish, Patrick J., *The Catholic Community in the Seventeenth and Eighteenth Centuries*. Helicon History of Ireland (Dublin, 1981).

Clear, Caitríona, *Social Change and Everyday Life in Ireland, 1850–1922* (Manchester University Press, 2007).

Coulter, H., *West of Ireland 1861*.

Daly, Mary, *Development of National School System 1831–1840*.

Danaher, Kevin:
  (1) *In Ireland Long Ago*. Dublin 1962.
  (2) Some Marriage Customs and their Regional Distribution in Béaloideas Iml. VIII, (1942–1944).

Donohoe, Tony, *The Story of Crossmolina*, Dublin and Castlehill Donohoe, 2003.

Edgeworth, Maria, *The Absentee*, London 1896, p. 46.

Finlay, T.A. (S.J.),
  (1) Foxford and the Providence Woollen Mills Dublin *c*.1900.
  (2) Foxford: The Answer to Socialism in New Ireland Review, Vol. XIV, 1900.

Fitzpatrick, David, *Emigration, 1801–70*.

Forbes, John, *Memorandums made in Ireland in the Autumn of 1852*. 2 Vols. (London, 1853).

Forster, Edward, Report: Society of Friends, Transactions. Appendix III.

Griffith's Valuation.

Hall, S.C., *Retrospect of a Long Life* (London, 1883).

Handley, James Edward, *The Irish in Scotland, 1800–1845* (Cork UP, 1946).

Hayden, Tom (ed.), *Irish hunger, personal reflections on the legacy of the Famine* (Dublin, 1991).

Healy, John:
  (1) *No One shouted Stop (The Death of an Irish Town)* Mercier Press (Cork, 1968).
  (2) *Nineteen Acres*, Kenny Bookstores (Galway, 1978).

Hoban, Brendan, *Turbulent Diocese, The Killala Troubles, 1798–1848* (Dublin, 2011).

Johnson, James., *A Tour in Ireland* (1844).

Kerr, Barbara. Irish Seasonal Migration to Great Britain (1800–1838) in Irish Historical Studies III, 1942–43.

Kerr, Donal A., *Peel, Priests and Politics 1841–1846*. Oxford Historical Monographs. Clarendon Press, Oxford.

King, Carla and Conor McNamara, *New Perspectives on the Nineteenth Century* (Dublin, 2011).

Langan-Egan, M., Some Insights on Women in Mayo 1851–1881 in North Mayo Historical Journal, Vol. 2. 2002.

Larkin, Emmett, The Devotional Revolution in Ireland in American Historical Review, 77 (1972).

Lee, Joseph, J.,
  (1) *The Modernisation of Irish Society, 1848–?* (Dublin, 1973).
  (2) Women and the Church since the Famine in Women in *Irish Society: The Historical Dimension* (eds.) Margaret MacCurtain and Donncha Ó Corráin (Dublin, 1978).

Luddy, Maria, 'Women and work in the 19th and early 20th century', Whelan, B. *Women and Paid Work in Ireland, 1500–1930.*

MacCurtain, Margaret, 'Women, the Vote and Revolution' in *Women in Irish Society.*

MacGiolla Meidhre, Seán, 'Some Notes on Irish Farmhouses' in Béaloideas, Iml. VIII, 1938. West. Gresham Dublinn. d. 1834.

Maxwell, W.H., *Wild Sports in the West* (Dublin, 1834).

Meehan, Rosa, *The Story of Mayo*, Mayo County Council 2003.

Miller, D., Irish Catholics and The Great Famine in Journal of Social History (ix), 1975, pp 81–98

Moran, Gerard, 'Near Famine: The Crisis in the West of Ireland, 1879–1882', Irish Studies Review No. 18 (Spring 1997) pp 14–21.

Nichols, T.L., *Forty Years of American Life*, 1862.

Nicholson, Asenath, *Ireland's Welcome to the Stranger for the purpose of personally investigating the condition of the Poor of Ireland* (Dublin, 1847).

Annals of the Famine in Ireland in 1847, 1848 and 1849, 2nd Edition ed. by M. Murphy, 1998.

Noel, B.W., *A Short Tour through the Midland Counties of Ireland in the Summer of 1836* (1837).

O Corráin, Donnchadh and Ó Ríordáin Tomás, *Emancipation, Famine and Religion* (Dublin, 2011).

O Gráda, Cormac, 'Seasonal Migration and Post-Famine Adjustment in the West of Ireland' in Studia Hibernica, No. 13, 1973.

O'Neill, Kevin, *Family and Farm in pre-Famine Ireland*. University of Wisconsin Press (1984)

O'Neill, T.P., The Great Irish Famine (1845–1852) in Irish Ecc. Record. Vol. LXIX, (November, 1947).

Ó Súilleabháin, Aka known as Humphrey O'Sullivan, *Cinn-Lae Amhlaoibh Uí Shúilleabháin (The Diary of Humphrey O'Sullivan)* translated by Tomás de Bháldraithe (Mercier Press, Dublin and Cork, 1979).

Otway, Caesar, *Sketches in Erris and Tirawley* (Dublin, 1841).

Pim, Jonathan, *Transactions*.

Praeger, Robert Lloyd, *The Way that I went* (Dublin, 1937).

Saunder's *Newsletters*.

Schrier, A., *Ireland and the Amerian Emigration*, (Minneapolis, 1958).

Simms, W.D., Narrative of the Fifth and Sixth weeks of Wm. Forster's Visit to some distressed districts in Ireland (Dublin 1847).

Skinner, Emily, *A Woman on the Goldfields: Recollections of Emily Skinner*, (1854–1878) ed. by Edward Duyker (Melbourne University Press, 1995).

Society of Friends
(1) *Transactions of the Central Relief Committee during the Famine in Ireland 1846–1847* (Dublin, 1852).
(2) Applications for Relief 1845–1848, Public Record Office.

Strauss, E., *Irish Nationalism and British Democracy* (London, 1951).

TeBrake, Janet, 'Irish Peasant Women in Revolt: The Land League Years in Irish Historical Studies', Vol. xxviii, No. 109 (May 1992).

Tocqueville, Alexis de, *Journeys to England and Ireland* quoted in *Peel, Priests and Politics*, p. 191.

Trevelyan, C.E., *The Irish Crisis* (London, 1848).

Tuke, James H., Visit to Connaught in the Autumn of 1847– Society of Friends: Transactions, Appendix III.

Webb, Richard D., Deputation to Erris in 1848 in Society of Friends: Transactions.

Whelan, Bernadette, *Women and Paid Work in Ireland, 1500– 1930* (Dublin, 2000).

Whelan, Kevin, 'Pre- and Post-Famine Landscape Change' in C. Póirtéir (ed.) *The Great Irish Famine* (Dublin, 1995).

Wilde, Sir William, *Popular Irish Superstitions* (1849).

Winstanley, Ml., *Ireland and the Land Question, 1800–1922*, Lancaster Pamphlets, 2007.

Young, Arthur, *A Tour in Ireland*, Vols I and II (1776–1779).

Index

www.ingramcontent.com/pod-product-compliance
Lightning Source LLC
Chambersburg PA
CBHW072133270326
41931CB00010B/1750